Vikings and Vows

by

Anne E. White

Vikings and Vows

Cover photograph and design by Bryan White.

ISBN 978-1-990258-26-8

Viking Tales, by Jennie Hall

"These Norse stories have, to my thinking, three values... the love of truth, the hardy endurance, the faithfulness to plighted word, that make them a child's fit companions." (Jennie Hall, "Notes to Teachers")

"From a house you see a sooty roof, from a ship you see Valhalla." (Olaf the Tooth Thrall)

from "Nobody Knows"
by Walter de la Mare

Nobody knows what the Wind is,
  Under the height of the sky,
Where the hosts of the stars keep far away house
  And its wave sweeps by–
Just a great wave of the air,
  Tossing the leaves in its sea,
And foaming under the eaves of the roof
    That covers me.
And so we live under deep water,
  All of us, beasts and men,
And our bodies are buried down under the sand,
  When we go again;
And leave, like the fishes, our shells,
  And float on the Wind and away,
To where, o'er the marvellous tides of the air,
  Burns day.

Introduction and Study Notes

Fathers looked at their children and thought: "They are not learning much. What will make them brave and wise? What will teach them to love their country and old Norway? Will not the stories of battles, of brave deeds, of mighty men, do this?" (from ***Chapter One****)*

Who is Harald, and how do we know about him?

These stories are about Harald Fairhair (also known as Harald Halfdanson), the first king of Norway, who lived from about 850 A.D. until 930 A.D. What we know about him was passed down through the oral traditions (Sagas) of Iceland and Norway, and through written versions which began around 1230.

Why are we not reading the whole book?

Only Part One of the book (the Harald stories) is assigned to AmblesideOnline Year One (or Form IA) students. Part Two covers the stories of Eric the Red and Leif Ericson, which are read in Year Two (Form IB) from other books. This edition includes only the eleven chapters from Part One.

Has this book been adapted or changed?

Yes, in two ways. First, it has been very lightly edited to update punctuation and a few words, or to clarify where the original wording seemed to cause confusion. Second, Jennie Hall's explanatory notes about Norse life have been incorporated into the first two chapters, and also into later vocabulary notes.

Would you hire Olaf as a babysitter? (The issue of Viking values)

We may begin the book by feeling a bit sorry for Olaf the Tooth Thrall, but as we hear his stories of theft, destruction of property, and even murder, we (especially as adults) wonder what sort of values they are passing on to children. Then there is Harald's vow:

> But when the tables were gone and the horns were going around, [Harald] stood up and raised high a horn of ale and said loudly: "This horn of memory I drink in honor of my father, Halfdan, son of Gudrod, who sits now in Valhalla. And I vow that I will grind my father's foes under my heel."

As Charlotte Mason advises, teachers should keep the lessons and the narrations focused on the story, rather than "pointing a moral." Like Duke Richard in *The Little Duke*, though, listeners to these tales will have to sort out the good values they contain from darker themes of power and revenge (not to mention heavy consumption of alcohol). Children, even young ones, may notice ideas in the story that did not seem to worry the author: questions of liberty, enslavement, and the value of a person (why didn't Gyda want to marry Harald until he was a more powerful king?). Christian children may also have questions about the Norse religious beliefs.

Here are some practical teaching suggestions from the author.

"[Visual] materials for this study are not difficult of access...colored photographs of Norwegian landscape are becoming common in our art stores. There are good illustrations in the geographical works referred to in the book list. These could be copied upon the blackboard. There are three books beautifully illustrated in color that it will be possible to find only in large libraries,— "Coast of Norway," by Walton; "Travels in the Island of Iceland," by Mackenzie; "Voyage en Islande et au Gröenland," by J. P. Gaimard. If the landscape is studied from the point of view of formation, the images will be more accurate and more easily gained, and the study will have a general value that will continue past the reading of these stories into all work in geography.

"Trustworthy pictures of Norse houses and costumes are difficult to obtain. In "Viking Age" and "Story of Norway," by Boyesen (G. P. Putnam's Sons, New York), are many copies of Norse antiquities in the fashion of weapons, shield-bosses, coins, jewelry, wood-carving. These are, of course, accurate, but of little interest to children. Their chief value lies in helping the teacher to piece together a picture that she can finally give to her pupils. [Editor's note: Newer pictorial books such as Usborne's *Who Were the Vikings* or *Viking Raiders* can be put to good use here, even if, as Hall says, it is more for the benefit of the teacher than the student.]

"Metal-working and wood-carving were the most important arts of the Norse. If children study products of these arts and actually do some of the work, they will gain a quickened sympathy with the people and an appreciation of their power. They may, perhaps, make something to merely illustrate Norse work; for instance, a carved ship's-head, or a copper shield, or a wrought door-nail. But, better, they may apply Norse ideas of form and decoration and Norse processes in making some modern thing that they can actually use; for instance, a carved wood pin-tray or a copper match holder…

"Frequent drawn or painted illustration by the children of costumes, landscapes, houses, feast halls, and ships will help to make these images clear. But dramatization will do more than anything else for the interpreting of the stories and the characters. It would be an excellent thing if at last, through the dramatization and the handwork, the children should come into sufficient understanding and enthusiasm to turn skalds and compose songs in the Norse manner. This requires only a small vocabulary and a rough feeling for simple rhythm, but an intensity of emotion and a great vividness of image.

"These Norse stories have, to my thinking, three values. The men, with the crude courage and the strange adventures that make a man interesting to children, have at the same time the love of truth, the hardy endurance, the faithfulness to plighted word, that make them a child's fit companions."

In summary:

1. Look for a few good photographs that show the landscape of Norway and Iceland. Paintings might also be useful.
2. Also look for pictures (or museum exhibits) of things like houses and costumes. Don't expect young children to get too excited over illustrations of weapons or coins; but do at least look through some of these books or websites yourself, if only to familiarize yourself with the territory, and maybe to bookmark a few of the best pictures.
3. Be cautious, for various reasons, about taking on big craft projects like building a model ship or decorating a papier-mâché

helmet. As Hall points out, students could incorporate Norse designs or symbols into wood-carving or metal projects; or, more appropriately for this age, they could just do simple versions of carving or metal work, since those are "real" activities that are described in the stories. (The book also describes knitting, weaving, embroidering flags…not to mention hair care…)

4. Have the students create their own illustrations of the stories (perhaps concentrating more on the homes, ships, costumes, etc., rather than on the more violent events).
5. Hall suggests the use of drama, but also (perhaps more interestingly) proposes that children create their own Norse-style songs, perhaps about the stories, but also about things they have done and seen themselves.
6. Rather than over-emphasizing either the Norse religious beliefs, or the violence of some of the stories, look for ways to encourage the three Norse values that Hall points out: "the love of truth, the hardy endurance, the faithfulness to plighted word." "Hardy endurance" might be the most age-appropriate idea of the three; Hall mentions that Harald grew strong and healthy because he spent so much time playing out of doors.

Using the Examination Questions

The questions at the end have been created for this study, and are intended to be used with Charlotte Mason's end-of-term examination methods. Feel free to adapt them in whatever ways work best for your students.

Prologue: Heroes and Houses, Sagas and Skalds

Introduction

When people put on plays, they first have to "set the stage." This shows where the story takes place, and something about the people who will be in it. This chapter "sets the stage" for the stories that make up the rest of the book.

There is one thing here that can be a bit confusing. The Icelandic storytellers and skalds we hear about in this chapter told the stories of their own heroes, such as King Harald Fairhair—but those people lived in the country of Norway. The "Norse" people are those whose families first came from Norway, even if they were living in Iceland or somewhere else.

Much of the setting, though, such as the way their houses were built, and the tradition of storytellers, will be the same no matter which of the countries we are talking about.

Vocabulary

carded: preparing wool for spinning by cleaning and untangling it

flitted: moved swiftly and lightly

knoll: small hill or mound

applause: praise for the performance

vellum: also called **parchment**

bower: the women's part of the house; or, in a wealthy person's home, a lady's bedroom.

thralls: slaves, also called bondservants

People, Places, Events

Iceland: Can you find Iceland on a map? Look for Norway, too, as it is the home of our hero Harald. Are Iceland and Norway far away from your own country?

Reading

Part One

Iceland is a little country far north in the cold sea. Men found it and went there to live more than a thousand years ago. During the warm season they used to fish and make fish-oil and hunt seabirds and gather feathers and tend their sheep and make hay. But the winters were long and dark and cold. Men and women and children stayed in the house and **carded** and spun and wove and knit. A whole family sat for hours around the fire in the middle of the room. That fire gave the only light. Shadows **flitted** in the dark corners. Smoke curled along the high beams in the ceiling. The children sat on the dirt floor close by the fire. The grown people were on a long narrow bench that they had pulled up to the light and warmth. Everybody's hands were busy with wool. The work left their minds free to think and their lips to talk. What was there to talk about? The summer's fishing, the killing of a fox, a voyage to Norway. But the people grew tired of this little gossip. Fathers looked at their children and thought:

"They are not learning much. What will make them brave and wise? What will teach them to love their country and old Norway? Will not the stories of battles, of brave deeds, of mighty men, do this?"

So, as the family worked in the red firelight, the father told of the kings of Norway, of long voyages to strange lands, of good fights. And in farmhouses all through Iceland these old tales were told over and over until everybody knew them and loved them.

Some men could sing and play the harp. This made the stories all the more interesting. People called such men "skalds," and they called their songs "sagas."

Part Two

Every midsummer there was a great meeting. Men from all over Iceland came to it and made laws. During the day there were rest times, when no business was going on. Then some skald would take his harp and walk to a large stone or a **knoll** and stand on it and begin a song of some brave deed of an old Norse hero. At the first sound of the harp and the voice, men came running from all directions, crying out:

"The skald! The skald! A saga!"

They stood about for hours and listened. They shouted **applause**. When the skald was tired, some other man would come up from the crowd and sing or tell a story. As the skald stepped down from his high position, some rich man would rush up to him and say:

"Come and spend next winter at my house. Our ears are thirsty for song."

So the best skalds traveled much and visited many people. Their songs made them welcome everywhere. They were always honored with good seats at a feast. They were given many rich gifts. Even the King of Norway would sometimes send across the water to Iceland, saying to some famous skald:

"Come and visit me. You shall not go away empty-handed. Men say that the sweetest songs are in Iceland. I wish to hear them."

These tales were not written. Few men wrote or read in those days. Skalds learned songs from hearing them sung. At last people began to write more easily. Then they said:

"These stories are very precious. We must write them down to save them from being forgotten."

After that many men in Iceland spent their winters in writing books. They wrote on sheepskin; **vellum**, we call it. Many of these old vellum books have been saved for hundreds of years, and are now in museums in Norway. Some leaves are lost, some are torn, all are yellow and crumpled. But they are precious. They tell us all that we know about that olden time. There are the very words that the men of Iceland wrote so long ago–stories of kings and of battles and of ship-sailing. Some of those old stories I have told in this book.

Part Three: About Norse Houses

In a rich Norseman's home were many buildings. The finest and largest was the great feast hall. Next were the **bower**, where the women worked, and the guest house, where visitors slept. Besides these were storehouses, stables, workshops, a kitchen, [and] a sleeping-house for **thralls**.

All these buildings were made of heavy, hewn logs, covered with tar to fill the cracks and to keep the wood from rotting. The ends of the logs, the door-posts, the peaks of gables, were carved into shapes of men and animals and were painted with bright colors.

These buildings were close together, often set around the four sides of a square yard. That yard was a busy and pleasant place, with men and women running across from one building to another. Sometimes a high fence with one gate went around all this, and only the tall, carved peaks of roofs showed from the outside.

Narration and Discussion

Think about the place where you live. What is the same as a Norse house? What is different?

"… these old tales were told over and over until everybody knew them and loved them." Do you have any storytellers in your family? What are your favourite stories?

Chapter One: The Baby

Introduction

In this chapter, we meet Harald as a newborn, and also learn something more about Norse houses and naming traditions.

In Other News

If you are following the AO Bible reading schedule, you will be reading this week about Joseph's dreams (Genesis 37:1-11). It might be interesting to compare them to the dream Harald's mother had.

Vocabulary

limbs: branches

witnesses: those who watch to see that a paper is properly signed or a ceremony is carried out (like a wedding)

sprinkled the baby: This ritual of sprinkling/naming is called *ausa vatni*. The original book includes a drawing of King Halfdan holding the baby while a servant holds a bowl of water before him.

own: acknowledge, recognize

People, Places, Events

King Halfdan: also called Halfdan the Black; the father of Harald. He is not the king over all Norway (as we will hear later), but only the eastern part of the country.

Reading

Part One

King Halfdan lived in Norway long ago. One morning his queen said to him:

"I had a strange dream last night. I thought that I stood in the grass before my bower. I pulled a thorn from my dress. As I held it in my fingers, it grew into a tall tree. The trunk was thick and red as blood, but the lower **limbs** were fair and green, and the highest ones were white. I thought that the branches of this great tree spread so far that they covered all Norway and even more."

"A strange dream," said King Halfdan. "Dreams are the messengers of the gods. I wonder what they would tell us," and he stroked his beard in thought.

Some time after that a serving-woman came into the **feast hall** where King Halfdan was. She carried a little white bundle in her arms.

"My lord," she said, "a little son is just born to you."

"Ha!" cried the king, and he jumped up from the high seat and hastened forward until he stood before the woman.

"Show him to me!" he shouted, and there was joy in his voice.

The serving-woman put down her bundle on the ground and turned back the cloth. There was a little naked baby. The king looked at it carefully.

"It is a goodly youngster," he said, and smiled. "Bring **Ivar** and **Thorstein**."

They were captains of the king's soldiers. Soon they came.

"Stand as **witnesses**," Halfdan said.

Then he lifted the baby in his arms, while the old serving-woman brought a silver bowl of water. The king dipped his hand into it and **sprinkled the baby**, saying:

"I **own** this baby for my son. He shall be called Harald. My naming gift to him is ten pounds of gold."

Then the woman carried the baby back to the queen's room. [*omission*] The queen looked at him and smiled and remembered her dream and thought:

"That great tree! Can it be this little baby of mine?"

Part Two: About Feast Halls

The feast hall was long and narrow, with a door at each end. Down the middle of the room were flat stones in the dirt floor. Here the fires burned. In the roof above these fires were holes for the smoke to go out, but some of it blew about the hall, and the walls and rafters were stained with it. But it was pleasant wood smoke, and the Norsemen did not dislike it. There were no large windows in a feast hall or in any other Norse building. High up under the eaves or in the roof itself were narrow slits that were called wind's-eyes. There was no glass in them, for the Norsemen did not know how to make it; but there were, instead, covers made of thin, oiled skin. These were put into the wind's-eyes in stormy weather. There were covers, too, for the smoke-holes. The only light came through these narrow holes, so on dark days the people needed the fire as much for light as for warmth.

Part Three: About Names

In those olden days a man did not have a surname that belonged to everyone in his family. Sometimes there were two or three men of the same name in a neighborhood. That caused trouble. People thought of two ways of making it easy to tell which man was being spoken of. Each was given a nickname. Suppose the name of each was Haki. One would be called Haki the Black because he had black hair. The other would be called Haki the Ship-chested because his chest was broad and strong. These nicknames were often given only for the fun of it. Most men had them,—Eric the Red, Leif the Lucky, Harald Fairhair, Rolf Go-afoot. The other way of knowing one Haki from the other was to tell his father's name. One was Haki, Eric's son. The other was Haki, Halfdan's son. If you speak these names quickly, they sound like Haki Ericsson and Haki Halfdansson. After a while they were written like that, and men handed them on to their sons and daughters. Some names that we have nowadays have come down to us in just that way—Swanson, Anderson, Peterson, Jansen. [*omission*]

Narration and Discussion

Why did the king "sprinkle" the baby? Does it sound like anything people do with new babies nowadays?

Do you have a nickname? Do you like it?

Something to do: The Norse houses had windows made of "thin, oiled skin." Year One students may have read *Little House in the Big Woods*. In her later book *On the Banks of Plum Creek*, which is AO Free Reading in Year Three, Laura Ingalls Wilder remembers living in a dugout house that had a "greased-paper window." Perhaps the closest thing you might have to this would be baking parchment, or waxed paper. What if you were to tape a piece of one of those to a cardboard frame, or just hold it in your hand, and try to look through it? Do you think it would work well as a window? Is it waterproof? There is an interesting YouTube video about this, called "Making greased paper windows."

Chapter Two: The Tooth Thrall

Introduction

Harald, now an active and curious boy, asks his "thrall" Olaf for the story behind a favourite large rock.

[Warning for sensitive children: Olaf tells Harald a story about a warrior who jumped to his death so that he could go to Valhalla.]

In Other News

If you are reading *Trial and Triumph*, this week's scheduled reading is "Patrick: Missionary to the Irish." Like Joseph in the Bible, and Olaf the thrall, Patrick was enslaved in another country. You might want to look for similarities or differences in their stories.

Vocabulary

he cut his first tooth: his first tooth appeared

tooth thrall: A slave who was "given" to a boy in celebration of his first tooth, to watch over him and teach him.

welded: joined together by melting metal

runes: an ancient kind of writing. In a note at the beginning of *The Hobbit*, J. R. R. Tolkien explains that "Runes were old letters originally used for cutting or scratching on wood, stone, or metal, and so were thin and angular."

fiord: a narrow inlet of the sea between cliffs

dagger: knife

mead: an alcoholic drink made with honey

People, Places, Events

Olaf: a thrall of King Halfdan's, originally from Denmark. We will find out more about Olaf through the stories he tells in the following chapters.

Thor: In Norse mythology, Thor was one of the major gods, and the son of **Odin**. He was the god of war, lightning, and thunder, and is shown holding a hammer.

Asgard: the home of the Norse gods

Valhalla: the place where brave Viking warriors go when they die

Aegir: Aegir is the Norse god of the sea, but Olaf's story is about a Viking warrior who had the same name.

Reading

Part One

When Harald was seven months old **he cut his first tooth**. Then his father said:

"All the young of my herds, lambs and calves and colts, that have been born since this baby was born, I this day give to him. I also give to him this thrall, **Olaf**. These are my tooth-gifts to my son."

The boy grew fast, for as soon as he could walk about he was out of doors most of the time. He ran in the woods and climbed the hills and waded in the creek. He was much with his **tooth thrall**, for the king had said to Olaf:

"Be ever at his call."

Now this Olaf was full of stories, and Harald liked to hear them.

"Come out to Aegir's Rock, Olaf, and tell me stories," he said almost every day.

So they started off across the hills. The man wore a long, loose coat of white wool, belted at the waist with a strap. He had on coarse shoes and leather leggings. Around his neck was an iron collar **welded** together so that it could not come off. On it were strange marks, called **runes**, that said:

"Olaf, thrall of Halfdan."

Harald's clothes were [brighter than Olaf's]. A cape of gray velvet hung from his shoulders. It was fastened over his breast with great gold buckles. When it waved in the wind, a scarlet lining flashed out, and the bottom of a little scarlet jacket showed. His feet and legs were covered with gray woolen tights. Gold lacings wound around his legs from his shoes to his knees. A band of gold held down his long, yellow hair.

It was a wild country that these two were walking over. They were climbing steep, rough hills. Some of them seemed made all of rock, with a little earth lying in spots. Great rocks hung out from them, with trees growing in their cracks. Some big pieces had broken off and rolled down the hill.

"**Thor** broke them," Olaf said. "He rides through the sky and hurls his hammer at clouds and at mountains. That makes the thunder and the lightning and cracks the hills. His hammer never misses its aim, and it always comes back to his hand and is eager to go again."

Part Two

When they reached the top of the hill they looked back. Far below was a soft, green valley. In front of it the sea came up into the land and made a **fiord**. On each side of the fiord high walls of rock stood up and made the water black with shadow. All around the valley were high hills with dark pines on them. Far off were the mountains. In the valley were Halfdan's houses around their square yard.

"How little our houses look down there!" Harald said. "But I can almost–yes, I can see the red dragon on the roof of the feast hall. Do you remember when I climbed up and sat on his head, Olaf?"

He laughed and kicked his heels and ran on.

At last they came to Aegir's Rock and walked up on its flat top. Harald went to the edge and looked over. A ragged wall of rock reached down, and two hundred feet below was the black water of the fiord. Olaf watched him for a while, then he said:

"No whitening of your cheek, Harald? Good! A boy that can face the fall of Aegir's Rock will not be afraid to face the war flash when he is a man."

"Ho, I am not afraid of the war flash now," cried Harald.

He threw back his cape and drew a little **dagger** from his belt.

"See!" he cried; "does this not flash like a sword? And I am not afraid. But after all, this is a baby thing! When I am eight years old I will have a sword, a sharp tooth of war."

He swung his dagger as though it were a long sword. Then he ran and sat on a rock by Olaf.

"Why is this Aegir's Rock?" he asked.

"You know that **Asgard** is up in the sky," Olaf said. "It is a wonderful city where the golden houses of the gods are in the golden grove. A high wall runs all around it. In the house of **Odin**, the All-father, there is a great feast hall larger than the whole earth. Its name is **Valhalla**. It has five hundred doors. The rafters are spears. The roof is thatched with shields. Armor lies on the benches. In the high seat sits Odin, a golden helmet on his head, a spear in his hand. Two wolves lie at his feet. At his right hand and his left sit all the gods and goddesses, and around the hall sit thousands and thousands of men, all the brave ones that have ever died.

"Now it is good to be in Valhalla; for there is **mead** there better than men can brew, and it never runs out. And there are skalds that sing wonderful songs that men never heard. And before the doors of Valhalla is a great meadow where the warriors fight every day and get glorious and sweet wounds and give many. And all night they feast, and their wounds heal. But none may go to Valhalla except warriors that have died bravely in battle. Men who die from sickness go with women and children and cowards to Niflheim. There Hela, who is queen, always sneers at them, and a terrible cold takes hold of their bones, and they sit down and freeze.

"Years ago **Aegir** was a great warrior. Aegir the Big-handed, they called him. In many a battle his sword had sung, and he had sent many warriors to Valhalla. Many swords had bit into his flesh and left marks there, but never a one had struck him to death. So his hair grew white and his arms thin. There was peace in that country then, and Aegir sorrowed, saying:

"'I am old. Battles are still. Must I die in bed like a woman? Shall I not see Valhalla?'

"Now thus did Odin say long ago:

"'If a man is old and is come near death and cannot die in fight, let him find death in some brave way and he shall feast with me in Valhalla.'

"So one day Aegir came to this rock.

"'A deed to win Valhalla!' he cried.

"Then he drew his sword and flashed it over his head and held his shield high above him, and leaped out into the air and died in the water of the fiord."

"Ho!" cried Harald, jumping to his feet. "I think that Odin stood up before his high seat and welcomed that man gladly when he walked through the door of Valhalla."

"So the songs say," replied Olaf, "for skalds still sing of that deed all over Norway."

Narration and Discussion

There should be much to discuss after a story like this! One big question is: what does it mean to be brave? Are there other ways to show courage without having to fight?

Are there places (like Aegir's rock) near your home that make you curious to know their stories? How could you find out about them?

Something to do: *"How little our houses look down there!" Harald said.* Have you ever been high up and looked down on big things that seemed quite small? Could you tell about or draw what you saw?

Something not to do: Please be very cautious about dramatizing this story. For obvious reasons.

Chapter Three: Olaf's Farm

Introduction

Olaf tells about the adventures of his earlier life.

Vocabulary

a-viking: to take a boat to some unprotected village or farm, and raid or plunder it: that is, to steal food or treasure, and sometimes to fight or cause damage as well.

I made her for only twenty oars: A ship that required only twenty oars would not have been very big.

foes: enemies

tiller: a lever for steering a boat (attached to the **rudder**)

drinking-horn: an animal horn, polished and used as a drinking cup

harry: carry out attacks; harass

smithy: workshop where metal is shaped

a great din: a loud noise

stingy: selfish, not generous

Bring in the table: Jennie Hall writes, "Before a meal thralls brought trestles into the feast hall and set them before the benches. Then they laid long boards across from trestle to trestle. These narrow tables stretched all along both sides of the hall. People sat at the outside edge only. So the thralls served from the middle of the room. They put baskets of bread and wooden platters of meat upon these bare boards. At the end of the meal they carried out tables and all, and the drinking-horns went round in a clean room."

crane over the fire: a way to hang the cooking pot

I drink this to your health: A friendly or respectful thing people say when they are drinking together; making a toast

I heard a cuckoo today: a cuckoo's call is a sign of spring

saucy: rude, smart-mouthed

Better With Pictures

But I stayed that spring and built me a boat: Photographs of Viking ships can be found online by searching for terms such as "Viking dragon boat" or "dragon ship."

People, Places, Events

Denmark: Can you find this on the map, along with Iceland and Norway? How might Olaf have sailed from Denmark to Norway?

Reading

Part One

At another time Harald asked:

"What is your country, Olaf? Have you always been a thrall?"

The thrall's eyes flashed.

"When you are a man," he said, "and go **a-viking** to **Denmark**, ask men whether they ever heard of Olaf the Crafty. There, far off, is my country, across the water. My father was Gudbrand the Big. Two hundred warriors feasted in his hall and followed him to battle. Ten sons sat at meat with him, and I was the youngest. One day he said:

"'You are all grown to be men. There is not elbow-room here for so many chiefs. The eldest of you shall have my farm when I die. The rest of you, off a-viking!'

"He had three ships. These he gave to three of my brothers. **But I stayed that spring and built me a boat. I made her for only twenty oars** because I thought few men would follow me; for I was young, fifteen years old. I made her in the likeness of a dragon. At the prow I carved the head with open mouth and forked tongue thrust out. I painted the eyes red for anger.

"'There, stand so!' I said, 'and glare and hiss at my **foes**.'

"In the stern I curved the tail up almost as high as the head. There I put the pilot's seat and a strong **tiller** for the **rudder**. On the breast and sides I carved the dragon's scales. Then I painted it all black and on the tip of every scale I put gold. I called her 'Waverunner.' There she sat on the rollers, as fair a ship as I ever saw.

"The night that it was finished I went to my father's feast. After the meats were eaten and the mead-horns came round, I stood up from my bench and raised my **drinking-horn** high and spoke with a great voice:

"'This is my vow: I will sail to Norway and I will **harry** the coast and fill my boat with riches. Then I will get me a farm and will winter in that land. Now who will follow me?'

"'He is but a boy,' the men said. 'He has opened his mouth wider than he can do.'

"But others jumped to their feet with their mead-horns in their hands. Thirty men, one after another, raised their horns and said: "'I will follow this lad, and I will not turn back so long as he and I live!'"

Part Two: Olaf Continues His Story

"On the next morning we got into my dragon and started. I sat high in the pilot's seat. As our boat flashed down the rollers into the water I made this song and sang it:

"'The dragon runs.
Where will she steer?
Where swords will sing,
Where spears will bite,
Where I shall laugh.'

"So we harried the coast of Norway. We ate at many men's tables uninvited. Many men we found overburdened with gold. Then I said:

"'My dragon's belly is never full,' and on board went the gold.

"Oh! it is better to live on the sea and let other men raise your crops and cook your meals. A house smells of smoke, a ship smells of frolic. From a house you see a sooty roof, from a ship you see Valhalla.

"Up and down the water we went to get much wealth and much frolic. After a while my men said: "'What of the farm, Olaf?'

"'Not yet,' I answered. 'Viking is better for summer. When the ice comes, and our dragon cannot play, then we will get our farm and sit down.'

"At last the winter came, and I said to my men: "'Now for the farm. I have my eye on one up the coast a way in King Halfdan's country.'

"So we set off for it. We landed late at night and pulled our boat up on shore and walked quietly to the house. It was rather a wealthy farm, for there were stables and a storehouse and a **smithy** at the sides of the house. There was but one door to the house. We went to it, and I struck it with my spear.

"'Hello! Ho! Hello!' I shouted, and my men made **a great din**.

"At last some one from inside said: "'Who calls?'

"'I call,' I answered. 'Open! or you will think it Thor who calls,' and I struck my shield against the door so that it made a great clanging.

"The door opened only a little, but I pushed it wide and leaped into the room. It was so dark that I could see nothing but a few sparks on the hearth. I stood with my back to the wall; for I wanted no sword reaching out of the dark for me.

"'Now start up the fire,' I said.

"'Come, come!' I called, when no one obeyed. 'A fire! This is cold welcome for your guests.'

"My men laughed. "'Yes, a **stingy** host! He acts as though he had not expected us.'

"But now the farmer was blowing on the coals and putting on fresh wood. Soon it blazed up, and we could see about us. We were in a little feast hall, with its fire down the middle of it. There were benches for twenty men along each side. The farmer crouched by the fire, afraid to move. On a bench in a far corner were a dozen people huddled together."

Part Three

"'Ho, thralls!' I called to them. '**Bring in the table**. We are hungry.'

"Off they ran through a door at the back of the hall. My men came in and lay down by the fire and warmed themselves, but I set two of them as guards at the door.

"'Well, friend farmer,' laughed one, 'why such a long face? Do you not think we shall be merry company?'

"'We came only to cheer you,' said another. 'What man wants to spend the winter with no guests?'

"'Ah!' another then cried out, sitting up. 'Here comes something that will be a welcome guest to my stomach.'

"The thralls were bringing in a great pot of meat. They set up a **crane over the fire** and hung the pot upon it, and we sat and watched it boil while we joked. At last the supper began. The farmer sat gloomily on the bench and would not eat, and you cannot wonder; for he saw us putting potfuls of his good beef and basket-loads of bread into our big mouths. When the tables were taken out and the mead-horns came round, I stood up and raised my horn and said to the farmer:

"'You would not eat with us. You cannot say no to half of my ale. **I drink this to your health**.'

"Then I drank half of the hornful and sent the rest across the fire to the farmer. He took it and smiled, saying: "'Since it is to my health,

I will drink it. I thought that all this night's work would be my death.'

"'Oh, do not fear that!' I laughed, 'for a dead man sets no tables.'

"So we drank and all grew merrier. At last I stood up and said:

"'I like this little taste of your hospitality, friend farmer. I have decided to accept more of it.'

"My men roared with laughter.

"'Come,' they cried, 'thank him for that, farmer. Did you ever have such a lordly guest before?'

"I went on:

"'Now there is no fun in having guests unless they keep you company and make you merry. So I will give out this law: that my men shall never leave you alone. Hakon there shall be your constant companion, friend farmer. He shall not leave you day or night, whether you are working or playing or sleeping. Leif and Grim shall be the same kind of friends to your two sons.'

"I named nine others and said: 'And these shall follow your thralls in the same way. Now, am I not careful to make your time go merrily?'

"So I set guards over every one in that house. Not once all that winter did they stir out of sight of some of us. So no tales got out to the neighbors. Besides, it was a lonely place, and by good luck no one came that way. Oh! that was fat and easy living."

Part Four

"Well, after we had been there for a long time, Hakon came in to the feast one night and said: '**I heard a cuckoo today**!'

"'It is the call to go a-viking,' I said.

"All my men put their hands to their mouths and shouted. Their eyes danced. Big Thorleif stood up and stretched himself.

"'I am stiff with long sitting,' he said. 'I itch for a fight.'

"I turned to the farmer.

"'This is our last feast with you,' I said.

"'Well,' he laughed, 'this has been the busiest winter I ever spent, and the merriest. May good luck go with you!'

"'By the beard of Odin!' I cried; 'you have taken our joke like a man.'

"My men pounded the table with their fists.

"'By the hammer of Thor!' shouted Grim. 'Here is no stingy

coward. He is a man fit to carry my drinking-horn, the horn of a sea-rover and a sword-swinger. Here, friend, take it,' and he thrust it into the farmer's hand. 'May you drink heart's-ease from it for many years. And with it I leave you a name, "Sif the Friendly." I shall hope to drink with you sometime in Valhalla.'

"Then all my men poured around that farmer and clapped him on the shoulder and piled things upon him, saying:

"'Here is a ring for Sif the Friendly.'

"'And here is a bracelet.'

"'A sword would not be ashamed to hang at your side.'

"I took five great bracelets of gold from our treasure chest and gave them to him.

"The old man's eyes opened wide at all these things, and at the same time he laughed.

"'May Odin send me such guests every winter!' he said.

"Early next morning we shook hands with our host and boarded the 'Waverunner' and sailed off.

"'Where shall we go?' my men asked.

"'Let the gods decide,' I said, and tossed up my spear.

"When it fell on the deck it pointed up-shore, so I steered in that direction. That is the best way to decide, for the spear will always point somewhere, and one thing is as good as another. That time it pointed us into your father's ships. They closed in battle with us and killed my men and sunk my ship and dragged me off a prisoner. They were three against one, or they might have tasted something more bitter at our hands. They took me before King Halfdan.

"'Here,' they said, 'is a rascal who has been harrying our coasts. We sunk his ship and men, but him we brought to you.'

"'A robber viking?' said the king, and scowled at me.

"I threw back my head and laughed.

"'Yes. And with all your fingers it took you a year to catch me.'

"The king frowned more angrily.

"'**Saucy**, too?' he said. 'Well, thieves must die. Take him out, Thorkel, and let him taste your sword.'

"Your mother, the queen, was standing by. Now she put her hand on his arm and smiled and said:

"'He is only a lad. Let him live. And would he not be a good gift for our baby?'

"Your father thought a moment, then looked at your mother and smiled.

"'Soft heart!' he said gently to her; then to Thorkel, 'Well, let him go, Thorkel!'

"Then he turned to me again, frowning. 'But, young sharp-tongue, now that we have caught you we will put you into a trap that you cannot get out of. Weld an iron collar on his neck.'

"So I lived and now am your tooth thrall. Well, it is the luck of war. But by the chair of Odin, I kept my vow!"

"Yes!" cried Harald, jumping to his feet. "And had a joke into the bargain. Ah! sometime I will make a brave vow like that."

Narration and Discussion

Why did young Olaf become a robber-viking?

Harald says to Olaf, "Sometime I will make a brave vow like that." Do you think he will? Can you think of any other stories where someone made a vow? (Students who enjoy longer books might like *Ballet Shoes* by Noel Streatfeild, in which three adopted sisters vow "to try and put our name into history books, because it's our very own…")

Creative narration: You are Sif the farmer, and a friend (not a robber) comes to visit. Tell (or act out) what happened over the winter.

Chapter Four: Olaf's Fight With Havard

Introduction

Olaf tells Harald another story from his going-a-viking days.

In Other News

Most of Olaf's adventures were about looking for treasure—and he seemed to be very good at it (at least until he got caught by the king).

If you are following the AO Bible reading schedule, you will be reading about another view of treasure (Luke 12:13-34).

Vocabulary

shut into their beds: The author says, "Around the sides of the feast hall were "shut-beds." They were like big boxes with doors opening into the hall. On the floor of this box was straw with blankets thrown over it. The people got into these beds and closed the doors and so shut themselves in. Olaf's men could have set heavy things against these doors or have put props against them. Then the people could not have got out; for on the other side of the bed was the thick outside wall of the feast hall, and there were no windows in it."

We shall all drink in Valhalla tonight: We're going to die.

Sloven!: Slob!

People, Places, Events

King Havard: seems to have been the king of another of the Norse kingdoms, possibly on one of the islands

Reading

At another time Harald said: "Tell me of a fight, Olaf. I want to hear about the music of swords."

Olaf's eyes blazed.

"I will tell you of our fight with **King Havard**," he said.

"One dark night we had landed at a farm. We left our 'Waverunner' in the water with three men to guard her. The rest of us went into the house. The farmer met us at the door, but he died by Thorkel's sword. The others we **shut into their beds**. The door at each end of the hall we had barred on the inside so that nobody could surprise us. We were busy going through the cupboards and shouting at our good luck. But suddenly we heard a shout outside:

"'Thor and Havard!'

"Then there was a great beating at the doors.

"'He has two hundred fighters with him,' said Grim; 'for we saw his ships last night. Thirty against two hundred! **We shall all drink in Valhalla tonight**.'

"'Well,' I cried, 'Odin shall have no unwilling guest in me.'

"'Nor in me,' cried Hakon.

"'Nor in me,' shouted Thorkel.

"And that shout went all around, and we drew out our swords and caught up our shields.

"'Hot work is ahead of us,' said Hakon. 'Besides, we must leave none of this mead for Havard. Lend a hand, some one.'

"Then he and another pulled out a great tub that sat on the floor of the cupboard.

"'I drink to Valhalla to-night,' cried Thorkel the Thirsty, and he plunged his horn deep into the tub.

"When he brought it up, his sleeve was dripping and the sweet mead was running over from the horn.

"'**Sloven**!' cried Hakon, and he struck Thorkel with his fist and knocked him over into the cupboard.

"He fell against the wooden wall at the back, and a carved panel swung open behind him. He dropped down head first. In a minute he put his head out of the hole again. We all stood staring.

"'I think it is a secret passage,' he said.

"'We will try it,' I answered in a whisper. 'Throw dirt on the fire. It must be dark.'

"So we dug up dirt from the earth floor and smothered the fire. All this time there was a terrible shouting and hammering at the doors, but they were of heavy logs and stood.

"'I with four more will guard this door,' I said, pointing to the east end.

"Immediately four men stepped to my side.

"'And I will guard the other,' Hakon said, and four went with him.

"'The rest of you, down the hole!' I said. 'Close the door after you. If luck is with us we will meet at the ships. Now Thor and our good swords help us! Quick! The doors are giving way.'

"So we ten men stood at the doors and held back the king's soldiers. It was dark in the room, and the people out of doors could not tell how many were inside. Few were eager to be the first in.

"'Thirty swords are waiting in there to eat up the first man,' we heard some one say.

"We chuckled at that.

"But the king stood in the very doorway and fought. Our five swords held him back for a long time, but at last he pushed in, and his men poured after him. We ran back and hid behind some tubs in a dark corner. The king's men went groping about and calling, but they did not find us. The room was full of shouting and running and sword-clashing; for in the dark and the noise the men could not tell their own soldiers. More than one fell by his friend's sword. When it was less crowded about the doorway, I whispered:

"'Follow me in double line. We will make for the ships. Keep close together.'

"So that double line of men, with swords swinging from both sides, ran out through the dark. Swords struck out at us, and we struck back. Men ran after us shouting, but our legs were as good as theirs. But I and Hakon and one other were all that reached the ship. There we saw our 'Waverunner' with sail up and bow pointing to open sea. We swam out to her and climbed aboard. Then the men swung the sail to the wind, and we moved off. Even as we went, a spear whizzed through the air, and Hakon fell dead; for the king and all his men were running to the shore.

"'After them!' they were shouting.

"Then we heard the king call to the men in his boats lying out in the water: 'Row to shore and take us in.'

"Thorkel was standing by my side. At that he laughed and said:

"'They do not answer. He left but a handful to guard his ships. They tasted our swords. And we went aboard and broke the oars and threw the sails into the water. It will be slow going for Havard tonight.'

"Then he turned to the shore and sang out loudly:

"'King Havard's ships are dead:
Olaf's dragon flies.
King Havard stamps the shore:
Olaf skims the waves.
King Havard shakes his fist.
Olaf turns and laughs.'

"That was the end of our meeting with King Havard."

Narration and Discussion

Who do you think is the hero of Olaf's story? (Is there one?)

Did anything about this story make you laugh?

For further thought: Why do you think Harald enjoys stories like this?

Creative narration: Thorkel made up a song to tell about the fight with King Havard. Could you make up a song or poem, using the same pattern, to tell about something you have seen? Here is an example.

> The lazy dog naps in the kitchen doorway.
>
> The cat stands near and hisses.
>
> The dog lifts up his head.
>
> The cat makes a great leap over the dog.
>
> The dog shakes his head.
>
> The cat turns and laughs.

Chapter Five: "Foes'-fear"

Introduction

Harald is growing and learning to do many new things. In this story, he goes out to find a spear handle, but ends up fighting a wolf.

Vocabulary

lance: spear

bellows: a tool used for blowing air into a fire

chasms [ka-zms]: gaps in the earth; ravines

haft: this usually means handle; but since Harald is driving the handle itself into the haft of the spear point, it means the bottom of it.

People, Places, Events

Ivar the Far-goer: Ingvar the Far-Travelled, who even claimed to have killed a dragon while on his travels.

Reading

Part One

Every day the boy Harald heard some such story of war or of the gods, until he could see Thor riding among the storm-clouds and throwing his hammer, until he knew that a brave man has many wounds, but never a one on his back. Many nights he dreamed that he himself walked into Valhalla, and that all the heroes stood up and shouted:

"Welcome! Harald Halfdanson!"

"Ah! the bite of the sword is sweeter than the kiss of your mother," he said to Olaf one day. "When shall I stand in the prow of a dragon and feast on the fight? I am hungry to see the world. **Ivar the Far-goer** tells me of the strange countries he has seen. Ah! we Vikings are great folk. There is no water that has not licked our boats' sides. This cape of mine came in a Viking boat from France. These cloak-pins came from a far country called Greece. In my father's house are golden cups from Rome, away on the southern sea. Every land pours rich things into our treasure-chest. Ivar has been to a strange country where it is all sand and is very hot. The people call their country Arabia. They have never heard of Thor or Odin. Ivar brought beautiful striped cloth from there, and wonderful, sweet-smelling waters. Oh! when shall the white horses of the sea lead me out to strange lands and glorious battles?"

Part Two

But Harald did something besides listen to stories. Every morning he was up at sunrise and went with a thrall to feed the hunting dogs. Thorstein taught him to swim in the rough waters of the fiord. Often he went with the men a-hunting in the woods, and learned to ride a horse, and pull a bow, and throw a **lance**. Ivar taught him to play the harp and to make up songs. He went much to the smithy, where the warriors mended their helmets and made their spears and swords of iron and bronze. At first he only watched the men or worked the **bellows**, but soon he could handle the tongs and hold the red-hot iron, and after a long time he learned to use the hammer and to shape metal.

One day he made himself a spear-head. It was two feet long and sharp on both edges. While the iron was hot he beat into it some runes. When the men in the smithy saw the runes they opened their eyes wide and looked at the boy, for few Norsemen could read.

"What does it say?" they asked.

"It is the name of my spear-point, and it says, 'Foes'-fear,'" Harald said. "But now for a handle."

Part Three

It was winter and the snow was very deep. So Harald put on his skis and started for a wood that was back from shore. Down the mountains he went, twenty, thirty feet at a slide, leaping over **chasms** a hundred feet across. In his scarlet cloak he looked like a flash of fire. The wind shot past him howling. His eyes danced at the fun.

"It is like flying," he thought and laughed. "I am an eagle. Now I soar," as he leaped over a frozen river.

He saw a slender ash [tree] growing on top of a high rock.

"That is the handle for 'Foes'-fear,'" he said.

The rock stood up like a ragged tower, but he did not stop because of the steep climb. He threw off his skis and thrust his hands and feet into holes of the rock and drew himself up. He tore his jacket and cut his leather leggings and scratched his face and bruised his hands, but at last he was on the top. Soon he had chopped down the tree and had cut a straight pole ten feet long and as big around as his arm. He went down, sliding and jumping and tearing himself on the sharp stones. With a last leap he landed near his skis. As he did so a lean wolf jumped and snapped at him, snarling. Harald shouted and swung his pole. The wolf dodged, but quickly jumped again and caught the boy's arm between his sharp teeth. Harald thought of the spear-point in his belt. In a wink he had it out and was striking with it. He drove it into the wolf's neck and threw him back on the snow, dead.

"You are the first to feel the tooth of 'Foes'-fear,'" he said, "but I think you will not be the last."

Then without thinking of his torn arm he put on his skis and went leaping home. He went straight to the smithy and smoothed his pole and drove it into the **haft** of the spear-point. He hammered out a gold band and put it around the joining place. He made nails with beautiful heads and drove them into the pole in different places.

"If it is heavy it will strike hard," he said.

Then he weighed the spear in his hand and found the balancing point and put another gold band there to mark it.

Thorstein came in while he was working.

"A good spear," he said.

Then he saw the torn sleeve and the red wound beneath.

"Hello!" he cried. "Your first wound?"

"Oh, it is only a wolf-scratch," Harald answered.

"By Thor!" cried Thorstein, "I see that you are ready for better wounds. You bear this like a warrior."

"I think it will not be my last," Harald said.

Narration and Discussion

How does Harald show that he is learning to be brave?

"He knew that a brave man has many wounds, but never a one on his back." What could this mean?

Creative narration #1: What are some things that Harald has learned to do? What things have you learned to do or make? What things are you still working on? What would else you like to learn or do or make?

> "Up and be doing, whether at work or play."
> (Charlotte Mason, *Ourselves Book I*, p. 20)

Creative narration #2: *"Ah! the bite of the sword is sweeter than the kiss of your mother," he said to Olaf one day.* This is the last we ever hear of Olaf. What do you think might have happened to him after Harald grew up?

Chapter Six: Harald is King

Introduction

Harald suddenly becomes king in his father's place, and he makes a serious vow.

Vocabulary

kinsmen: relatives

People, Places, Events

Gudrod: also called Gudrød the Hunter or Gudrød the Magnificent; a Norse king from the early 9th century A.D., and Harald's grandfather.

Reading

Part One

Now when Harald was ten years old, his father, King Halfdan, died. An old book that tells about Harald says that then "he was the biggest of all men, the strongest, and the fairest to look upon." That [was said] about a boy ten years old! But boys grew fast in those days for they were out of doors all the time, running, swimming, leaping on skis, and hunting in the forest [*omission*].

So now King Halfdan was dead and buried, and Harald was to be king. But first he must "drink his father's funeral ale."

"Take down the [colourful] tapestries that hang in the feast hall," he said to the thralls. "Put up black and gray ones. Strew the floor with pine branches. Brew twenty tubs of fresh ale and mead. Scour every dish until it shines."

Then Harald sent messengers all over that country to his **kinsmen** and friends.

"Bid them come in three months' time to drink my father's funeral ale," he said. "Tell them that no one shall go away empty-handed."

Part Two

So in three months men came riding up at every hour. Some came in boats. But many had ridden far through mountains, swimming rivers; for there were few roads or bridges in Norway. On account of that hard ride, no women came to the feast.

At nine o'clock in the night the feast began. The men came walking in at the west end of the hall. The great bonfires down the middle of the room were flashing light on everything. The clean smell of this wood-smoke and of the pine branches on the floor was pleasant to the guests. Down each side of the hall stretched long, backless benches, with room for three hundred men. In the middle of each side rose the high seat, a great carved chair on a platform. All along behind the benches were the black and gray draperies. Here hung the shields of the guests; for every man, when he was given his place, turned and hung his shield behind him and set his tall spear by it. So on each wall there was a long row of [*omission*] shields, red and green and yellow, and all shining with gold or bronze trimmings. And higher up there was another row of gleaming spear-points. Above the hall the rafters were carved and gaily painted, so that dragons seemed to be crawling across, or eagles seemed to be swooping down.

The guests walked in laughing and talking with their big voices so that the rafters rang. They made the hall look all the brighter with their clothes of scarlet and blue and green, with their flashing golden bracelets and head-bands and sword-scabbards, with their flying hair of red or yellow.

Across the east end of the hall was a bench. When the men were all in, the queen, Harald's mother, and the women who lived with her, walked in through the east door and sat upon this bench.

Then thralls came running in and set up the long tables before the benches. Other thralls ran in with large steaming kettles of meat. They put big pieces of this meat into platters of wood and set it before the men. They had a few dishes of silver. These they put before the guests at the middle of the tables; for the great people sat here near the high seats.

When the meat came, the talking stopped; for Norsemen ate only twice a day, and these men had had long rides and were hungry. Three or four persons ate from one platter and drank from the same big bowl of milk. They had no forks, so they ate from their fingers and threw the bones under the table among the pine branches. Sometimes they took knives from their belts to cut the meat.

When the guests sat back satisfied, Harald called to the thralls:

"Carry out the tables."

So they did and brought in two great tubs of mead and set one at each end of the hall. Then the queen stood up and called some of her women. They went to the mead tubs. They took the horns, when the thralls had filled them, and carried them to the men with some merry word [*omission*].

The women were beautiful, moving about the hall. The queen wore a trailing dress of blue velvet with long flowing sleeves. She had a short apron of striped Arabian silk with gold fringe along the bottom. From her shoulders hung a long train of scarlet wool embroidered in gold. White linen covered her head. Her long yellow hair was pulled around at the sides and over her [dress], and was fastened under the belt of her apron. As she walked, her train made a pleasant rustle among the pine branches. She was tall and straight and strong. Some of her younger women wore no linen on their heads and had their white arms bare, with bracelets shining on them. They, too, were tall and strong.

All the time men were calling across the fire to one another asking news or telling jokes and laughing.

An old man, Harald's uncle, sat in the high seat on the north side. That was the place of honor. But the high seat on the south side was empty; for that was the king's seat. Harald sat on the steps before it.

The feast went merrily until long after midnight. Then the thralls took some of the guests to the guest house to sleep, and some to the beds around the sides of the feast hall. But some men lay down on the benches and drew their cloaks over themselves.

Part Three

On the next night there was another feast. Still Harald sat on the step before the high seat. But when the tables were gone and the horns were going around, he stood up and raised high a horn of ale and said loudly:

"This horn of memory I drink in honor of my father, Halfdan, son of **Gudrod**, who sits now in Valhalla. And I vow that I will grind my father's foes under my heel."

Then he drank the ale and sat down in the king's high seat, while all the men stood up and raised their horns and shouted:

"King Harald!"

And some cried: "That was a brave vow."

And Harald's uncle called out: "A health to King Harald!"

And they all drank it.

Then a man stood up and said:

"Hear my song of King Halfdan!" for this man was a skald.

"Yes, the song!" shouted the men, and Harald nodded his head.

So the skald took down his great harp from the wall behind him and went and stood before Harald. The bottom of the harp rested on the floor, but the top reached as high as the skald's shoulders. The brass frame shone in the light. The strings were some of gold and some of silver. The man struck them with his hand and sang of King Halfdan, of his battles, of his strong arm and good sword, of his death, and of how men loved him.

When he had finished, King Harald took a bracelet from his arm and gave it to him, saying:

"Take this as thanks for your good song."

The guests stayed the next day and at night there was another feast.

When the mead horns were going around, King Harald stood up and spoke:

"I said that no man should go away empty-handed from drinking my father's funeral ale."

He beckoned the thralls, and they brought in a great treasure-chest and set it down by the high seat. King Harald opened it and took out rich gifts–capes and sword-belts and beautiful cloth and bracelets and gold cloak-pins. These he sent about the hall and gave something to every man. The guests wondered at the richness of his gifts.

"This young king has an open hand," they said, "and deep treasure-chests."

After breakfast the next morning the guests went out and stood by their horses ready to go, but before they mounted, thralls brought a horn of mead to each man. That was called the stirrup-horn, because after they drank it the men put their feet to the stirrups and sprang upon their horses and started. King Harald and his people rode a little way with them.

All men said that that was the richest funeral feast that ever was held.

Narration and Discussion

How does Harald show a different kind of bravery in this chapter?

What do you think of his vow? (A Bible verse to consider: Matthew 5:43-44)

Creative narration: "Here hung the shields of the guests; for every man, when he was given his place, turned and hung his shield behind him and set his tall spear by it." Illustrate this scene, and add your own shield to the ones on the wall. What colours or symbols would you use?

Chapter Seven: Harald's Battle

Introduction

Harald, though still a young king, is ready to fight off those who threaten his kingdom.

Vocabulary

forges: hearths (fires) used for heating metal so that it can be hammered and shaped

anvils: iron or steel blocks on which metal is hammered

coats of mail: armour

standard-bearer: flag-carrier

rivets: metal fasteners

ermine: a stoat (like a weasel); its winter fur is traditionally used on royal robes

provision wagons: food-supply wagons

frolic: party

hazels: hazel twigs, used to mark out the battlefield

hel-shoes (*helskór*): shoes placed on the feet of dead warriors so they could walk to Valhalla. (Sometimes spelled **hell-shoes**.)

People, Places, Events

King Haki: or Hake; a famous Norse sea-king

Reading

Part One

Now King Halfdan had many foes. When he was alive they were afraid to make war upon him, for he was a mighty warrior. But when Harald became king, they said:

"He is but a lad. We will fight with him and take his land."

So they began to make ready. King Harald heard of this and he laughed and said:

"Good! 'Foes'-fear' is thirsty, and my legs are stiff with much sitting."

He called three men to him. To one he gave an arrow, saying:

"Run and carry this arrow north. Give it into the hands of the master of the next farm, and say that all men are to meet here within two weeks from this day. They must come ready for war and mounted on horses. Say also that if a man does not obey this call, or if he receives this arrow and does not carry it on to his next neighbor, he shall be outlawed from this country, and his land shall be taken from him."

He gave arrows to the other two men and told them to run south and east with the same message.

So all through King Harald's country men were soon busy mending helmets and polishing swords and making shields. There was blazing of **forges** and clanging of **anvils** all through the land.

Part Two

On the day set, the fields about King Harald's house were full of men and horses. After breakfast a horn blew. Every man snatched his weapons and jumped upon his horse. Men of the same neighborhood stood together, and their chief led them. They waited for the starting horn.

This did not look like [armies today]. There were no uniforms. Some men wore helmets, some did not. Some wore **coats of mail**, but others wore only their jackets and tights of bright-colored wool. But at each man's left side hung a great shield. Over his right shoulder went his sword-belt and held his long sword under his left hand. Above most men's heads shone the points of their tall spears. Some men carried axes in their belts. Some carried bows and arrows. Many had ram's horns hanging from their necks.

King Harald rode at the front of his army with his **standard-bearer** beside him. Chain-armor covered the king's body. A red cloak was thrown over his shoulders. On his head was a gold helmet with a dragon standing up from it. He carried a round shield on his left arm. The king had made that shield himself. It was of brass. The **rivets** were of silver, with strangely shaped heads. On the back of Harald's horse was a red cloth trimmed with the fur of **ermine**.

King Harald looked up at his standard and laughed aloud.

"Oh, War-lover," he cried, "you and I ride out on a [merry] journey."

A horn blew again and the army started. The men shouted as they went, and blew their ram's horns.

"Now we shall taste something better than even King Harald's ale," shouted one.

Another rose in his stirrups and sniffed the air.

"Ah! I smell a battle," he cried. "It is sweeter than those strange waters of Arabia."

So the army went merrily through the land. They carried no tents, they had no **provision wagons**.

"The sky is a good enough tent for a soldier," said the Norsemen. "Why carry provisions when they lie in the farms beside you?"

After two days King Harald saw another army on the hills.

"Thorstein," he shouted, "up with the white shield and go tell **King**

Haki to choose his battlefield. We will wait but an hour. I am eager for the **frolic**."

Part Three

So Thorstein raised a white shield on his spear as a sign that he came on an errand of peace. He rode near King Haki, but he could not wait until he came close before he shouted out his message and then turned and rode back.

"Tell your boy king that we will not hang back," Haki called after Thorstein.

King Harald's men waited on the hillside and watched the other army across the valley. They saw King Haki point and saw twenty men ride off as he pointed. They stopped in a patch of hazel and hewed with their axes.

"They are getting the **hazels**," said Thorstein.

"Audun," said King Harald to a man near him, "stay close to my standard all day. You must see the best of the fight. I want to hear a song about it after it is over."

This Audun was the skald who sang at the drinking of King Halfdan's funeral ale.

King Haki's men rode down into the valley. They drove down stakes all about a great field. They tied the hazel twigs to the stakes in a string. But they left an open space toward King Harald's army and one toward King Haki's. Then a man raised a white shield and galloped toward King Harald.

"We are ready!" he shouted.

At the same time King Haki raised a red shield. King Harald's men put their shields before their mouths and shouted into them. It made a great roaring war-cry.

"Up with the war shield!" shouted King Harald. "Horns blow!"

There was a blowing of horns on both sides. The two armies galloped down into the field and ran together. The fight had begun.

All that day long swords were flashing, spears flying, men shouting, men falling from their horses, swords clashing against shields.

"Victory flashes from that dragon," Harald's men said, pointing to the king's helmet. "No one stands before it." And, surely, before night came, King Haki fell dead under "Foes'-fear."

When he fell, a great shout went up from his warriors, and they turned and fled. King Harald's men chased them far, but during the night [they] came back to camp. Many brought swords and helmets, and bracelets, or silver-trimmed saddles and bridles with them.

"Here is what we got from the foe," they said.

Part Four

The next morning King Harald spoke to his men: "Let us go about and find our dead."

So they went over all the battle-field. They put every man on his shield and carried him and laid him on a hill-top. They hung his sword over his shoulder and laid his spear by his side. So they laid all the dead together there on the hill-top. Then King Harald said, looking about:

"This is a good place to lie. It looks far over the country. The sound of the sea reaches it. The wind sweeps here. It is a good grave for Norsemen and Vikings. But it is a long road and a rough road to Valhalla that these men must travel. Let the nearest kinsman of each man come and tie on his **hel-shoes**. Tie them fast, for they will need them much on that hard road."

So friends tied shoes on the dead men's feet. Then King Harald said:

"Now let us make the mound."

Every man set to work with what tools he had and heaped earth over the dead until a great mound stood up. They piled stones on the top. On one of these stones King Harald made runes telling how these men had died.

After that was done King Harald said:

"Now set up the pole, Thorstein. Let every man bring to that pole all that he took from the foe."

So they did, and there was a great hill of things around it. Harald divided it into piles.

"This pile we will give to Thor in thanks for the victory," he said. "This pile is mine because I am king. Here are the piles for the chiefs, and these things go to the other men of the army."

So every man went away from that battle richer than he was before, and Thor looked down from Valhalla [*omission*] and was pleased.

The next morning King Harald led his army back. But on the way he met other foes, and had many battles, and did not lose one. The kings either died in battle or ran away, and Harald had their lands.

"He has kept his vow," men said, "and ground his father's foes under his heel."

So King Harald sat in peace for a while.

Narration and Discussion

Did King Harald keep his vow all by himself? What kind of help did he need?

Creative narration: We have not yet heard a song about this battle from Audun the skald. What do you think he might say?

Chapter Eight: Gyda's Saucy Message

Introduction

Those who complain there aren't enough girls in this story are compensated here. Harald hears of a young woman who is "fair and proud," but she unfortunately turns out to be a little *too* proud.

Vocabulary

make runes: write

herbs: plants used as medicine

wind's-eyes: windows (see note in **Chapter One**)

vikings: refers to raiders and robbers, not to Norse people in general

smart: hurt

put our heads between his knees: a required part of the loyalty ceremony

People, Places, Events

Gyda: Although history is blurred on Gyda's identity, she seems most closely identified with Ragnhild the Mighty, the daughter of **King Eirikr** (here called **King Eric**).

Harald Shockhead: also translated as "Harald Horrid-locks" (see *The Little Duke*, Chapter 8, Part 2). A nickname for Harald.

Reading

Part One

Now Harald heard men talk of Gyda, the daughter of **King Eric**.

"She is very beautiful," they said, "but she is very proud, too. She can both read and **make runes**. No other woman in the world knows so much about **herbs** as she does. She can cure any sickness. And she is proud of all this!"

Now when King Harald heard that, he thought to himself:

"Fair and proud. I like them both. I will have her for my wife."

So he called his uncle, Guthorm, and said:

"Take rich gifts and go to Gyda's [father] and tell him that I will marry Gyda."

So Guthorm and his men came to that house and they told [King Harald's] message to [her father]. Gyda was standing near, weaving a rich cloak. She heard the speech. She came up and said, holding her head high and curling her lip:

"I will not waste myself on a king of so few people. Norway is a strange country. There is a little king here and a little king there—hundreds of them scattered about. Now in Denmark there is but one great king over the whole land. And it is so in Sweden. Is no one brave enough to make all of Norway his own?"

She laughed a scornful laugh and walked away. The men stood with open mouths and stared after her. Could it be that she had sent that saucy message to King Harald? They looked at her [father]. He was chuckling in his beard and said nothing to them. They started out of the house in anger. When they were at the door, Gyda came up to them again and said:

"Give this message to your King Harald for me: I will not be his wife unless he puts all of Norway under him for my sake."

Part Two

So Guthorm and his men rode homeward across the country. They did not talk. They were all thinking. At last one said:

"How shall we give this message to the king?"

"I have been thinking of that," Guthorm said; "his anger is no little thing."

It was late when they rode into the king's yard; for they had ridden slowly, trying to make some plan for softening the message, but they had thought of none.

"I see light through the **wind's-eyes** of the feast hall," one said.

"Yes, the king keeps feast," Guthorm said. "We must give our message before all his guests."

So they went in with very heavy hearts. There sat King Harald in the high seat. The benches on both sides were full of men. The tables had been taken out, and the mead-horns were going round.

"Oh, ho!" cried King Harald. "Our messengers! What news?"

Then Guthorm said: "This Gyda is a bold and saucy girl, King Harald. My tongue refuses to give her message."

The king stamped his foot.

"Out with it!" he cried. "What does she say?"

"She says that she will not marry so little a king," Guthorm answered.

Harald jumped to his feet. His face flushed red. Guthorm stretched out his hand.

"They are not my words, O King; they are the words of a silly girl."

"Is there any more?" the king shouted. "Go on!"

"She said: 'There is one king in Denmark and one king in Sweden. Is there no man brave enough to make himself king of all Norway? Tell King Harald that I will not marry him unless he puts all of Norway under him for my sake.'"

The guests sat speechless, staring at Guthorm. All at once the king broke into a roar of laughter.

"By the hammer of Thor!" he cried, "that is a good message. I thank you, Gyda. Did you hear it, friends? King of all Norway! Why, we are all stupids. Why did we not think of that?"

Then he raised his horn high.

"Now hear my vow. I say that I will not cut my hair or comb it until I am king of all Norway. That I will be, or I will die."

Then he drank off the horn of mead, and while he drank it, all the men in the hall stood up and waved their swords and shouted and shouted. That old hall in all its two hundred years of feasts had not heard such a noise before.

"Ah, Harald!" Guthorm cried, "surely Thor in Valhalla smiled when he heard that vow."

The men sat all night talking of that wonderful vow.

Part Three

On the very next day King Harald sent out his war-arrows. Soon a great army was gathered. They marched through the country north and south and east and west, burning houses and fighting battles as they went. People fled before them, some to their own kings, some inland to the deep woods and hid there. But some went to King Harald and said:

"We will be your men."

"Then take the oath, and I will be friends with you," he said.

The men took off their swords and laid them down and came one by one and knelt before the king. They [each] said:

"From this day, Harald Halfdanson, I am your man. I will serve you in war. For my land I will pay you taxes. I will be faithful to you as my king."

Then Harald said: "I am your king, and I will be faithful to you."

Many kings took that oath and thousands of common men. Of all the battles that Harald fought, he did not lose one.

Part Four

Now for a long time the king's hair and beard had not been combed or cut. They stood out around his head in a great bushy mat of yellow. At a feast one day when the jokes were going round, Harald's uncle said:

"Harald, I will give you a new name. After this you shall be called

Harald Shockhead. As my naming gift I give you this drinking-horn."

"It is a good name," laughed all the men.

After that all people called him Harald Shockhead.

During these wars, whenever King Harald got a country for his own, this is what he did. He said:

"All the marshland and the woodland where no people live is mine. For his farm every man shall pay me taxes."

Over every country he put some brave, wise man and called him [the] Earl [of that place]. He said to the earls:

"You shall collect the taxes and pay them to me. But some you shall keep for yourselves. You shall punish any man who steals or murders or does any wicked thing. When your people are in trouble they shall come to you, and you shall set the thing right. You must keep peace in the land. I will not have my people troubled with robber-vikings."

The earls did all these things as best they could; for they were good strong men. The farmers were happy. They said:

"We can work on our farms with peace now. Before King Harald came, something was always wrong. The **vikings** would come and steal our gold and our grain and burn our houses, or the king would call us to war. Those little kings are always fighting. It is better under King Harald."

Part Five

But the chiefs, who liked to fight and go a-viking, hated King Harald and his new ways. One of these chiefs was [named] Solfi. He was a king's son. Harald had killed his father in battle. Solfi had been in that battle. At the end of it he fled away with two hundred men and got into ships.

"We will make that Shockhead **smart**," he said.

So they harried the coast of King Harald's country. They filled their ships with gold. They ate other men's meals. They burned farmhouses behind them. The people cried out to the earls for help. So the earls had out their ships all the time trying to catch Solfi, but he was too clever for them.

In the spring, [Solfi] went to a certain king, Audbiorn, and said to him:

"Now, there are two things that we can do. We can become this

Shockhead Harald's thralls, [and] we can kneel before him and **put our heads between his knees**. Or else we can fight. My father thought it better to die in battle than to be any man's thrall. How is it? Will you join with my cousin Arnvid and me against this young Shockhead?"

"Yes, I will do it," said the king.

Narration and Discussion

What is Harald's new vow? Do you think he will be able to keep it?

Why were some people happy under Harald's rule, but not others?

Creative narration: Can you imagine making a vow not to comb your hair? What are some difficulties you might get into? (Somewhat along the same lines: "The Radish Cure" in *Mrs. Piggle-Wiggle.*)

Chapter Nine: The Sea Fight

Introduction

King Harald's enemies have gathered against him, but he is prepared for the fight—especially if it means winning Gyda's hand in marriage. (And being able to comb his hair again.)

Vocabulary

prow: the part of a ship's **bow** (front portion) which is above water

veer: turn suddenly

cables: ropes

stern: back part of the ship

furled: rolled up

gunwale: the upper edge of the side of a ship (where, in later times, one might have rested guns or cannons)

prow to prow: nose to nose

People, Places, Events

King Arnvid: a king who fought in the Second Battle of Solskjel against Harald Fairhair in 870.

Ran: Ran was the wife of Aegir, the Norse god of the sea.

Reading

Part One

Many men felt as Solfi did. So when King Audbiorn and **King Arnvid** sent out their war arrows, a great host gathered. All men came by sea. Two hundred ships lay at anchor in the fiord, looking like strange swimming animals because of their high carved **prows** and bright paint. There were red and gold dragons with long necks and curved tails. Sea-horses reared out of the water. Green and gold snakes coiled up. Sea-hawks sat with spread wings ready to fly. And among all these curved necks stood up the tall, straight masts with the long yardarms swinging across them holding the looped-up sails.

When the starting horn blew, and their sails were let down, it was like the spreading of hundreds of curious flags. Some were striped black and yellow or blue and gold. Some were white with a black raven or a brown bear embroidered on them, or blue with a white sea-hawk, or black with a gold sun. Some were edged with fur. As the wind filled the [*omission*] sails, and the ships moved off, the [kings'] men waved their hands to the women on shore and sang:

"To the sea! To the sea!
The wind in our sail,
The sea in our face,
And the smell of the fight.
After ship meets ship,
In the quarrel of swords
King Harald shall lie

In the caves under sea

And Norsemen shall laugh."

Part Two

In the prow stood men leaning forward and sniffing the salt air with joy. Some were talking of King Harald.

"Yesterday he had a hard fight," they said. "Today he will be lying still, dressing his wounds and mending his ships. We shall take him by surprise."

They sailed near the coast. Solfi in his "Sea-hawk" was ahead, leading the way. Suddenly men saw his sail **veer** and his oars flash out. He had quickly turned his boat and was rowing back. He came close to King Arnvid and called:

"He is there, ahead. His boats are ready in line of battle. The fox has not been asleep."

King Arnvid blew his horn. Slowly his boats came into line with his "Sea-stag" in the middle. Again he blew his horn. **Cables** were thrown across from one prow to the next, and all the ships were tied together so that their sides touched. Then the men set their sails again and they went past a tongue of land into a broad fiord. There lay the long line of King Harald's ships with their fierce heads grinning and mocking at the newcomers. Back of those prows was what looked like a long wall with spots of green and red and blue and yellow and shining gold. It was the locked shields of the men in the bows, and over every shield looked fierce blue eyes. Higher up and farther back was another wall of shields; for on the half deck in the **stern** of every ship stood the captain with his shield-guard of a dozen men.

Arnvid's people had **furled** their sails and were taking down the masts, but the ships were still drifting on with the wind. The horn blew, and quickly every man sprang to his place in bow and stern. All were leaning forward with clenched teeth and widespread nostrils. They were clutching their naked swords in their hands. Their flashing eyes looked over their shields.

Part Three

Soon King Arnvid's ships crashed into Harald's line, and

immediately the men in the bows began to swing their swords at one another. The soldiers of the shield-guard on the high decks began to throw darts and stones and to shoot arrows into the ships opposite them.

So in every ship showers of stones and arrows were falling, and many men died under them or got broken arms or legs. Spears were hurled from deck to deck and many of them bit deep into men's bodies. In every bow men slashed with their swords at the foes in the opposite ship. Some jumped upon the **gunwale** to get nearer or hung from the prow-head. Some even leaped into the enemy's boat.

King Harald's ship lay **prow to prow** with King Arnvid's. The battle had been going on for an hour. King Harald was still in the stern on the deck. There was a dent in his helmet where a great stone had struck. There was a gash in his shoulder where a spear had cut. But he was still fighting and laughed as he worked.

"Wolf meets wolf to-day," he said. "But things are going badly in the prow," he cried. "Ivar fallen, Thorstein wounded, a dozen men lying in the bottom of the boat!"

He leaped down from the deck and ran along the gunwale, shouting as he went:

"Harald and victory!"

So he came to the bow and stood swinging his sword as fast as he breathed. Every time it hit a man of Arnvid's men. Harald's own warriors cheered, seeing him.

"Harald and victory!" they shouted, and went to work again with good heart.

Part Four

Slowly King Arnvid's men fell back before Harald's biting sword. Then Harald's men threw a great hook into that boat and pulled it alongside and still pushed King Arnvid's people back.

"Come on! Follow me!" cried Harald.

Then he leaped into King Arnvid's boat, and his warriors followed him.

"He comes like a mad wolf," King Arnvid's men said, and they turned and ran back below the deck.

Then Arnvid himself leaped down and stood with his sword raised.

"Can this young Shockhead make cowards of you all?" he cried.

But Harald's sword struck him, and he fell dead. Then a big, bloody Viking of King Arnvid leaped upon the edge of the ship and stood there. He held his drinking-horn and his sword high in his hands.

"**Ran** and not you, Shockhead, shall have them and me!" he cried, and leaped laughing into the water and was drowned.

Many other warriors chose the same death on that terrible day.

All along the line of boats men fought for hours. In some places the cables had been cut, and the boats had drifted apart. Ships lay scattered about two by two, fighting. Many boats sank, many men died, some fled away in their ships, and at the end King Harald had won the battle. So he had King Arnvid's country, and King Audbiorn's country. Many men took the [loyalty] oath and became his friends. All people were talking of his wonderful battles.

Narration and Discussion

How did Harald win the battle against these enemies?

What do you think he will do next?

For further discussion: *"He comes like a mad wolf," King Arnvid's men said.* Does that remind you of earlier chapters in the book?

Creative narration: What do you think of the men's sea song? Do you know any other good sea songs (perhaps not about fighting)? Here are some from the AO Folk Songs list: "Skye Boat Song"; "There's a Hole in the Bottom of the Sea"; "The Saucy Sailor." Perhaps that last one would be a good one for Harald to sing to Gyda. "I will cross the briny ocean, I will whistle and I'll sing; Since you have refused the offer, love, Another girl shall have the ring."

Chapter Ten: King Harald's Wedding

Introduction

After ten years of fighting (and tangled hair), Harald decides it is time to earn himself a new nickname.

Vocabulary

girdle: belt, sash

Better With Pictures

It is not hard to find online photographs of a "Viking wedding," because such weddings have become popular in recent years. However, most of the extra information on those websites will not be of interest to (or appropriate for) Year One students. The description given in this chapter would seem to be enough for students to create their own illustrations of the wedding.

Reading

Part One

It had taken King Harald ten years to fight so many battles. And all that time he had not cut his hair or combed it. Now he was feasting one day at an earl's house. Many people were there.

"How is it, friends?" Harald said. "Have I kept my vow?"

His friends answered:

"You have kept your vow. There is no king but you in all Norway."

"Then I think I will cut my hair," the king laughed.

So he went and bathed and put on fresh clothes. Then the earl cut his hair and beard, and combed them, and put a gold band about his head. Then he looked at [his hair] and said:

"It is beautiful, smooth, and yellow."

And all people wondered at the beauty of the king's hair.

"I will give you a new name," the earl said. "You shall no longer be called Shockhead. You shall be called 'Harald Fairhair.'"

"It is a good name," everybody cried.

Part Two

Then Harald said: "But I have another thing to do now. Guthorm, you shall take the same message to Gyda that you gave ten years ago."

So Guthorm went and brought back this answer from Gyda:

"I will marry the king of all Norway."

So when the wedding time came, Harald rode across the country to the home of Gyda's father, Eric. Many men followed him. They were all richly dressed in velvet and gold.

For three nights they feasted at Eric's house. On the next night Gyda sat on the cross-bench with her women. A long veil of white linen covered her face and head and hung down to the ground. After the mead-horns had been brought in, Eric stood up from his high seat and went down and stood before King Harald.

"Will you marry Gyda now?" he asked.

Harald jumped to his feet and laughed.

"Yes," he said. "I have waited long enough."

Then he stepped down from his high seat and stood by Eric. They walked about the hall. Before them walked thralls carrying candles. Behind them walked many of King Harald's great earls. Three times they walked around the hall. The third time they stopped before the cross-bench. King Harald and Eric stepped upon the platform, where the cross-bench was.

Eric gave a holy hammer to Harald, and it was like the hammer of Thor. Harald put it upon Gyda's lap, saying:

"With this holy hammer of Thor's, I, Harald, King of Norway, take you, Gyda, for my wife."

Then he took a bunch of keys and tied it to Gyda's **girdle**, saying:

"This is the sign that you are mistress of my house."

After that, Eric called out loudly:

"Now are Harald, King of Norway, and Gyda, daughter of Eric, man and wife."

Then thralls brought meat and drink in golden dishes. They were about to serve it to Gyda for the bride's feast, but Harald took the dish from them and said:

"No, I will serve my bride."

So he knelt and held the platter. When he did that his men shouted. Then they talked among themselves, saying:

"Surely Harald never knelt before. It is always other people who kneel to him."

When the bride had tasted the food and touched the mead-horn to her lips, she stood up and walked from the hall. All her women followed her, but the men stayed and feasted long.

Part Three

On the next morning at breakfast Gyda sat by Harald's side. Soon the king rose and said:

"Father-in-law, our horses stand ready in the yard. Work is waiting for me at home and on the sea. Lead out the bride."

So Eric took Gyda by the hand and led her out of the hall. Harald followed close. When they passed through the door Eric said:

"With this hand I lead my daughter out of my house and give her to you, Harald, son of Halfdan, to be your wife. May all the gods make you happy!"

Harald led his bride to the horse and lifted her up and set her behind his saddle and said: "Now this Gyda is my wife."

Then they drank the stirrup-horn and rode off.

"Everything comes to King Harald," his men said; "wife and land and crown and victory in battle. He is a lucky man."

Narration and Discussion

What was your favourite part of the wedding ceremony?

Why does Harald say that "work is waiting for me at home and on the sea?" Should the king of Norway have to work?

For further thought: People said that Harald was a "lucky man" for gaining so many good things. Do you think he was just lucky, or did he make his own luck?

Creative narration: What might the skalds sing about Harald and

Gyda's wedding?

Chapter Eleven: King Harald Goes West-Over-Seas

Introduction

In **Chapter Ten** we had our "happy ending," but now we find out that some people still did not live happily under Harald's rule. This chapter will lead us into the era of Norsemen who settled in new lands, such as Leif Ericson and "Big Rolf-go-afoot." We will learn more about each of them in AO Year Two (Form IB).

Vocabulary

say them nay: do or say anything against them

People, Places, Events

Big Rolf-go-afoot: the first ruler of Normandy, and the grandfather of Richard, *The Little Duke.* His name can be translated as Hrólfr the Walker; but he is also called Rollo.

the great French River: the Seine

Normandy: Normandy is now a part of France, but at that time (as you will read in *The Little Duke*), it was a "duchy," ruled over by a duke.

his sons' sons after him were kings of England: See *An Island Story*, chapter 24, "The Battle of Hastings."

Reading

Part One

Now many men hated King Harald. Many a man said:

"Why should he put himself up for king of all of us? He is no better than I am. Am I not a king's son as well as he? And are not many of us kings' sons? I will not kneel before him and promise to be his man. I will not pay him taxes. I will not have his earl sitting over me. The good old days have gone. This Norway has become a prison. I will go away and find some other place."

So hundreds of men sailed away. Some went to France and got land and lived there. **Big Rolf-go-afoot** and all his men sailed up **the great French River**, and won a battle against the French king himself. There was no way to stop the flashing of his battle-axes but to give him what he wanted. So the king made Rolf a duke, gave him broad lands, and gave him the king's own daughter for wife. Rolf called his country **Normandy**, for old Norway. He ruled it well and was a great lord, and **his sons' sons after him were kings of England**.

Other Norsemen went to Ireland and England and Scotland. They drew up their boats on the river banks. The people ran away before them and gathered into great armies that marched back to meet the Vikings in battle. Sometimes the Norsemen lost, but oftener they won, so that they got land and lived in those countries. Their houses sat in these strange lands like warriors' camps, and the Norsemen went among their new neighbors with hanging swords and spears in hand, ever ready for fight.

There are many islands north of Scotland. They are called the Orkneys and the Shetlands. They have many good harbors for ships. They are little and rocky and bare of trees. Wild sea-birds scream around them. On some of them a man can stand in the middle and see the ocean all about him. Now the Vikings sailed to these islands and were pleased.

"It is like being always in a boat," they said. "This shall be our home."

Part Two

So it went until all the lands round about were covered with Vikings. Norse carved and painted houses brightened the hillsides. Viking ships sailed all the seas and made harbor in every river. Norsemen's thralls plowed the soil and planted crops and herded cattle, and gold flowed into their masters' treasure-chests. Norse warriors walked up and down the land, and no man dared to **say them nay**.

These men did not forget Norway. In the summers they sailed back there and **harried** the coast. They took gold and grain and beautiful cloth back to their homes. In Norway they left burning houses and weeping women.

Every summer King Harald had out his ships and men and hunted these vikings. There are many little islands about Norway. They have crags and caves and deep woods. Here the vikings hid when they saw King Harald's ships coming. But Harald ran his boat into every creek and fiord and hunted in every cave and through all the woods and among the crags. He caught many men, but most of them got away and went home laughing at Harald. Then they came back the next summer and did the same deeds over again. At last King Harald said:

"There is but one thing to do. I must sail to these western islands and whip these robbers in their own homes."

Part Three

So he went with a great number of ships. He found men [as brave as those] he had brought from Norway. These Vikings had brought their old courage to their new homes. King Harald's fine ships were scarred by Viking stones and scorched by Viking fire. The shields of Harald's warriors had dents from Viking blows. Many of those men carried Viking scars all their lives. And many of King Harald's warriors walked the long, hard road to Valhalla, and feasted there with some of these very Vikings that had died in King Harald's battles. But after many hard fights on land and sea, after many men had died and many had fled away to other lands, King Harald won, and he made the men that were yet in the islands take the oath, and he left his earls to rule over them. Then he went back to Norway.

"He has done more than he vowed to do," people said. "He has not only whipped the Vikings, but he has got a new kingdom west-over-seas."

Then they talked of that dream that his mother had.

"King Harald was that great tree," they said. "The trunk was red with the blood of his many battles, but higher up the limbs were fair and green like this good time of peace. The topmost branches were white because Harald will live to be an old man. Just as that tree spread out until all of Norway was in its shade, and even more lands, so Harald is king of all this country and of the western islands. The many branches of that tree are the many sons of Harald, who shall be earls and kings in Norway, and their sons after them, for hundreds of years."

Narration and Discussion

Why did some people feel Norway had become a prison?

Why was it so difficult for King Harald to fight against the Norsemen who had settled in the western islands?

What was your favourite part of this book? What would you like (or not like) about living in Harald's time?

Examination Questions for *Viking Tales*

Choose one or more of these questions.

1. Tell a story about Harald's childhood.

2. Tell what you know about a Viking funeral or a Viking wedding.

3. How did Harald get to be king of all Norway?

The Little Duke, by Charlotte Mary Yonge

"Few names in history shine with so consistent a lustre as that of Richard; at first the little Duke, afterwards Richard *aux longues jambes* [of the long legs], but always Richard *sans peur* [the fearless]."

The Arrow and the Song

by Henry Wadsworth Longfellow

I shot an arrow into the air,
It fell to earth, I knew not where;
For, so swiftly it flew, the sight
Could not follow it in its flight.

I breathed a song into the air,
It fell to earth, I knew not where;
For who has sight so keen and strong,
That it can follow the flight of song?

Long, long afterward, in an oak
I found the arrow, still unbroke;
And the song, from beginning to end,
I found again in the heart of a friend.

Preface and Study Suggestions

Since those following the AmblesideOnline Curriculum will be reading *The Little Duke* with Year Two (Form IB) students, these notes are intended for the benefit of parents/teachers, rather than for children to use themselves. This is one of three books by Charlotte Yonge included in the AmblesideOnline curriculum. In Charlotte Mason's era, it was scheduled as "Reading" (supplementary fiction) in Form II (the upper elementary years).

Please don't expect children in Year Two to memorize the vocabulary lists, or understand all the historical events; young Richard often doesn't comprehend what's going on either. It's not even vital to the story that Richard, the "Little Duke," becomes the great-grandfather of William the Conqueror; but as his own father's name is William, that often causes confusion. You might want to set the stage, though, by explaining a little of how the some of the Norsemen (with whom Year Two students should already be familiar after reading *Viking Tales*) came to settle in the region of Normandy, which is now part of France. At the time of this story, their culture was still very much "Norse," although we are told that they were already forgetting their language. One of the issues that Richard faces is the reconciling of his Norse heritage, including violent sagas of revenge, with his family's recent conversion to Christianity.

The story starts on an autumn day in a rather cold castle. Richard is the young son of the Duke who rules Normandy; but he lives with another family both because the Duke is busy and because that was the custom (see the notes for **Chapter One**). On this day, he is anxiously waiting for his father to arrive on one of his too-rare visits.

Words and Names

> "Evelyn Payne-Ellis, whoever she might be, had provided portraits and a family tree, and had made no attempt, it seemed, to...'write forsoothly'. There were no 'by our Ladys', no 'nathelesses' [neverthelesses] or 'varlets'." (Josephine Tey, *Daughter of Time*)

Charlotte Yonge does tend to "write forsoothly": there is one actual "forsooth," in Chapter Five, and a "varlet" in Chapter Nine. Her vocabulary can be even more challenging today than was originally intended, as young readers (especially in North America) may not understand her use of then-common words such as "apartment" (room), "bidden" (ordered), or "embarked" (went on board); though many of these can be guessed at by their context. You might choose a couple of key words to teach before each reading, especially those that can be shown with a picture (e.g. "hauberk").

I have made very few edits to Yonge's text. Some words have been replaced (and noted) where the meaning has changed, or when a French term would have made things unnecessarily difficult. Some punctuation has been updated, but I have kept her use of capital letters where we would more commonly use lowercase (e.g. Castle, Knight).

Reading and Narrating

Charlotte Mason had a simple lesson plan: "Proper names are written on the blackboard, and then the children narrate what they have listened to." If the students can read, writing out names of main characters can be helpful (although the French names in this story may be difficult). A supplement, especially for younger or non-reading students, would be to keep track with some form of hand-drawn characters, such as paper dolls, or stick figures drawn on a white board.

The chapters of the novel are each divided in half, following the AO reading schedule. Most of the half-chapter lessons are also divided into two or more parts. These section breaks may be where you choose to stop and narrate, or to show a picture or map. You can also use the section breaks to divide the reading over multiple days.

Using the Examination Questions

As the book is scheduled over two terms, there are two sets of examination questions, which have been created for this study guide. Feel free to adapt them in whatever ways work best for your students.

Chapter One: The Silver Key (Part 1)

Introduction

This is a story about a real boy named Richard, who was born in the year 932 A.D. How long ago is that? About a thousand years, plus another hundred or so. Do you think boys (or girls) were much different a thousand years ago?

The book begins when Richard is ten years old. (The writer of the book guesses that he might be eight or nine, but if you do the math, he must be ten.) His father, Duke William, is the ruler of Normandy, which today is part of France, but which at that time was a separate kingdom; but because it was ruled not by a king but by a duke, it was called a **duchy**. (This is the first word in the book that many people will not know how to pronounce, but it's not that hard: "DUT-chee.")

Look for Normandy on a map of France: what about it do you notice? One important thing is that it's on the sea, and it includes islands as well as mainland territory. The other thing is that Normandy is very close to England, just across the English Channel; and while that is not important to Richard's story, it is something you will want to remember for later history lessons.

Young Richard doesn't live at home with his father; he is being brought up by a noble family called the de Centevilles (duh SAHN-tuh-VEELS), who live at the Castle of Bayeux (pronounced in French as bye-YUH; in British English, bay-YUH; and in the U.S., bye-you). The book says that Richard's mother was named Duchess Emma but that she has died. (History books give different stories and names for the Duke's wife, but we will go with this book's version.)

One thing that you do need to know is that Richard, his father, and the de Centevilles are not French at all. They are Normans, or North-Men, originally from Norway. Their parents and grandparents were Vikings, just like those in the *Viking Tales.* In fact, Duke William's father was "Rollo the Walker," or **Big Rolf-go-afoot** as he is called in the last chapter we read from *Viking Tales.* The King of France (the one just before the one you will hear about) had agreed to give Rollo and the Norsemen their own land, probably with the hope that they would settle down and not go out raiding other places, and that was pretty much what happened. In this story, one of the reasons Richard's father chooses the de Centeville family for him to live with is that they still speak the Norse language (instead of newfangled French) and can teach him all the stories about the old days in Norway. Sometimes that's a good thing, but it can also cause problems.

One other fact we do know about Richard is that when he grew up and got married, his great-grandson was a Norman ruler named William, who is known in English history as William the Conqueror. If you are following the AO history schedule for *An Island Story*, you will be reading about him soon.

So, we have young Richard who lives with the de Centeville family; and as the story opens on a rather cold and gloomy day, they are all getting ready for a visit from Duke William and some other Norman nobles. The Duke has some big troubles around the duchy, but those don't interest Richard much; he just wants the chance to spend time with his father, and tell him how he helped shoot the big stag that they're going to have for dinner.

Better With Pictures

You may want to look for illustrations or photos of life in a Norman castle, and try to pick out some of the items from the vocabulary list such as hearth, cauldron, trenchers. If you are following the AO reading schedule, in Week 7 you will be reading about "Real Castles" in *A Child's History of the World*, or "The Hardy Northmen" in *Discovery of New Worlds*. You might want to read "Real Castles" now instead of later on.

"The Hardy Northmen" is also interesting, as it gives a bit of background on who the Vikings were, and tells the story of Richard's grandfather Rollo.

Vocabulary

crypt: burying place

cathedral: large church

apartment: room

hearths: fireplaces

cauldrons: cooking pots

rushes: a marsh plant, gathered and used as a floor covering

trestles: frameworks to support a tabletop

drinking horns: polished horns of cattle, used as drinking cups

trenchers: Plates. Sort of. Early trenchers were made of stale bread, but these were made of wood.

chased: ornamented

steward: servant in charge of household affairs (like a butler)

venison: deer meat

stag of ten branches: a male deer with large antlers

shaft: arrow

haunch: part of the deer

slightly made: slim

vassal: one who serves another, not as a household servant but in the sense of loyalty and support (such as helping to fight enemies)

spit: a long metal rod pushed through meat so that it can be cooked over a fire

dress something else: Meant to be a joke. You can dress meat, and you can dress little boys, but not in the same way.

tunic: a piece of clothing similar to a long shirt, with or without sleeves

dagger: short sword or knife

venomous: poisonous, dangerous

Sagas: ballads, heroic tales

embattled: fortified, protected

pupil in chivalry: one who is learning to be a squire and then a knight

People, Places, Events

Dame Astrida / Fru Astrida / Lady Astrida (Yonge uses the names interchangeably): the mother of **Sir Eric de Centeville.** She oversees the castle servants and also cares for their "foster-son," young Richard. The de Centeville family also have a son named **Osmond**, who is about ten years older than Richard.

Osmond de Centeville (or Centville): We know that Osmond (Osmon, Osmund) was a real person. His uncle, **Bernard de Harcourt**, asked him to be tutor to Richard after the death of Duke William. It is also stated in one history book that Osmond rescued Richard from his captivity in Laon; but that book was published half a century after *The Little Duke*, and, for all we know, that author might have been using this book as his source!

Walter: a character we will hear more about later on.

Sigurd, Ragnar (Lodbrok): famous Viking warriors

their Prince: Duke William

Reading

Part One

On a bright autumn day, as long ago as the year 943, there was a great bustle in the **Castle of Bayeux** in **Normandy**.

The hall was large and low, the roof arched, and supported on thick short columns, almost like the **crypt** of a **Cathedral**; the walls were thick, and the windows, which had no glass, were very small, set in such a depth of wall that there was a wide deep window seat, upon which the rain might beat, without reaching the interior of the room. And even if it had come in, there was nothing for it to hurt, for the walls were of rough stone, and the floor of tiles. There was a fire at each end of this great dark **apartment**, but there were no chimneys over the ample **hearths**, and the smoke curled about in thick white folds in the vaulted roof, adding to the wreaths of soot, which made the hall look still darker.

The fire at the lower end was by far the largest and hottest. Great black **cauldrons** hung over it, and servants, both men and women, with red faces, bare and grimed arms, and long iron hooks, or pots and pans, were busied around it. At the other end, which was raised about three steps above the floor of the hall, other servants were engaged. Two young maidens were strewing fresh **rushes** on the floor; some men were setting up a long table of rough boards, supported on **trestles**, and then ranging upon it silver cups, **drinking horns**, and wooden **trenchers**.

Benches were placed to receive most of the guests, but in the middle, at the place of honour, was a high chair with very thick crossing legs, and the arms curiously carved with lions' faces and claws; a clumsy wooden footstool was set in front, and the silver drinking-cup on the table was of far more beautiful workmanship than the others, richly **chased** with vine leaves and grapes, and figures of little boys with goats' legs. If that cup could have told its story, it would have been a strange one, for it had been made long since, in the old Roman times, and been carried off from Italy by some Northman pirate.

From one of these scenes of activity to the other, there moved a stately old lady: her long thick light hair, hardly touched with grey, was bound round her head, under a tall white cap, with a band passing under her chin: she wore a long sweeping dark robe, with wide hanging sleeves, and thick gold earrings and necklace, which had possibly come from the same quarter as the cup. She directed the servants, inspected both the cookery and arrangements of the table, held council with an old **steward**, now and then looked rather anxiously from the window, as if expecting someone, and began to say something about fears that these loitering youths would not bring home the **venison** in time for Duke William's supper.

Presently, she looked up rejoiced, for a few notes of a bugle-horn were sounded; there was a clattering of feet, and in a few moments there bounded into the hall, a boy of about eight years old, his cheeks and large blue eyes bright with air and exercise, and his long light-brown hair streaming behind him, as he ran forward flourishing a bow in his hand, and crying out, "I hit him, I hit him! **Dame Astrida**, do you hear? 'Tis a **stag of ten branches**, and I hit him in the neck."

"You! my Lord Richard! you killed him?"

"Oh, no, I only struck him. It was Osmond's **shaft** that took him in the eye, and–Look you, **Fru Astrida**, he came thus through the wood, and I stood here, it might be, under the great elm with my bow thus"– And Richard was beginning to act over again the whole scene of the deer-hunt, but Fru, that is to say, **Lady Astrida**, was too busy to listen, and broke in with, "Have they brought home the **haunch**?"

"Yes, **Walter** is bringing it. I had a long arrow–"

A stout forester was at this instant seen bringing in the venison, and Dame Astrida hastened to meet it, and gave directions, little Richard following her all the way, and talking as eagerly as if she was attending to him, showing how he shot, how Osmond shot, how the deer bounded, and how it fell, and then counting the branches of its antlers, always ending with, "This is something to tell my father. Do you think he will come soon?"

Part Two

In the meantime two men entered the hall, one about fifty, the other, one or two-and-twenty, both in hunting dresses of plain leather, crossed by broad embroidered belts, supporting a knife, and a bugle-horn. The elder was broad-shouldered, sun-burnt, ruddy, and rather stern-looking; the younger, who was also the taller, was **slightly made**, and very active, with a bright keen grey eye, and merry smile. These were Dame Astrida's son, **Sir Eric de Centeville**, and her grandson, **Osmond**; and to their care Duke William of Normandy had committed his only child, Richard, to be fostered, or brought up.

It was always the custom among the Northmen, that young princes should thus be put under the care of some trusty **vassal**, instead of being brought up at home, and one reason why the Centevilles had been chosen by Duke William was, that both Sir Eric and his mother spoke only the old Norwegian tongue, which he wished young Richard to understand well, whereas, in other parts of the Duchy, the Normans had forgotten their own tongue, and had taken up [a dialect] which was the beginning of [modern] French.

On this day, Duke William himself was expected at Bayeux, to pay a visit to his son before setting out on a journey to settle the disputes between the Counts of Flanders and Montreuil, and this was the reason of Fru Astrida's great preparations. No sooner had she seen the haunch placed upon a **spit**, which a little boy was to turn before the fire, than she turned to **dress something else**, namely, the young

Prince Richard himself, whom she led off to one of the upper rooms, and there he had full time to talk, while she, great lady though she was, herself combed smooth his long flowing curls, and fastened his short scarlet cloth **tunic**, which just reached to his knee, leaving his neck, arms, and legs bare. He begged hard to be allowed to wear a short, beautifully ornamented **dagger** at his belt, but this Fru Astrida would not allow.

"You will have enough to do with steel and dagger before your life is at an end," said she, "without seeking to begin over-soon."

"To be sure I shall," answered Richard. "I will be called Richard of the Sharp Axe, or the Bold Spirit, I promise you, Fru Astrida. We are as brave in these days as the **Sigurds** and **Ragnars** you sing of! I only wish there were serpents and dragons to slay here in Normandy."

"Never fear but you will find even too many of them," said Dame Astrida; "there be dragons of wrong here and everywhere, quite as **venomous** as any in my **Sagas**."

"I fear them not," said Richard, but half understanding her, "if you would only let me have the dagger! But, hark! hark!" he darted to the window. "They come, they come! There is the banner of Normandy." Away ran the happy child, and never rested till he stood at the bottom of the long, steep, stone stair, leading to the **embattled** porch. Thither came the Baron de Centeville, and his son, to receive **their Prince**.

Part Three

Richard looked up at Osmond, saying, "Let me hold his stirrup," and then sprang up and shouted for joy, as under the arched gateway there came a tall black horse, bearing the stately form of the Duke of Normandy. His purple robe was fastened round him by a rich belt, sustaining the mighty weapon, from which he was called "William of the Long Sword," his legs and feet were cased in linked steel chain-work, his gilded spurs were on his heels, and his short brown hair was covered by his ducal cap of purple, turned up with fur, and a feather fastened in by a jewelled clasp. His brow was grave and thoughtful, and there was something both of dignity and sorrow in his face, at the first moment of looking at it, recalling [*omission*] that he had early lost his young wife, the Duchess Emma, and that he was beset by many cares and toils; but the next glance generally conveyed encouragement, so full of mildness were his eyes, and so kind the expression of his lips.

And now, how bright a smile beamed upon the little Richard, who, for the first time, paid him the duty of a **pupil in chivalry**, by holding the stirrup while he sprung from his horse. Next, Richard knelt to receive his blessing, which was always the custom when children met their parents. The Duke laid his hand on his head, saying, "God of His mercy bless thee, my son," and lifting him in his arms, held him to his breast, and let him cling to his neck and kiss him again and again, before setting him down, while Sir Eric came forward, bent his knee, kissed the hand of his Prince, and welcomed him to his Castle.

Narration and Discussion

What is it like when you have to wait all day for someone special to arrive at your house? What do you do to get ready for them?

Richard says, "I only wish there were serpents and dragons to slay here in Normandy." Fru Astrida responds, "Never fear but you will find even too many of them…" What do you think she means?

Creative narration: Drama? Illustrations? Perhaps a picture of Richard in his red tunic (but with no dagger)?

Chapter One: The Silver Key (Part 2)

Introduction

As the chapter continues, Duke William reminds young Richard not to be too enthusiastic about stories of old Norse battles and heroes, and especially those glorifying violence and vengeance. He also tells Richard (like any good father would!) to show a better attitude towards his school work.

Vocabulary

in the train: as followers (not actually in a train)

bidden: ordered

hauberk: a piece of armour covering the neck and shoulders

the expedition on which they were bound: The men will soon be heading out to discuss some business with other nobles who are not very friendly to them

restitution: repayment, compensation

the Grace: "Grace" is often a prayer to begin a meal, but at this banquet it ends the meal instead.

steeds: horses

parchment: sheets of thin material, made from animal skins, used instead of paper

clerk: A clerk was someone who used his reading and writing skills to serve the church, or another employer such as the King. Some clerks were scholars, but others (as Richard says) were more like secretaries.

vipers: snakes

feud: fight

contests: conflicts, fights

coronet: crown

in a fortnight's time: in about two weeks

People, Places, Events

Father Lucas: Richard's teacher

Throughout the book, you will hear names from Norse mythology, such as these:

Odin: the ruler of the gods, considered the god of war

Thor: another god of war

There are a number of nobles and rulers in the book, especially those referred to as **The Barons**. They include the following:

Count Arnulf of Flanders (often called The Fleming, because he was of the Flemish people)

Count Herluin II of Montreuil (also spelled Herlouin), who does not appear "onstage" in this story until quite near the end, but who seems to have been in the middle of quite a lot of the Normans' troubles

Count Bernard of Harcourt (often called The Dane)

Baron Rainulf of Ferrières

Duke Alan of Brittany (he does not appear in this chapter)

We hear of **King Hako of Norway**, also known as Haakon the Good; and **King Ethelstane** of England. (The author should probably have checked her history books more carefully, as Ethelstane had died and been succeeded by his half-brother **Edmund I**.) **King Alfred** of England is also mentioned; students may remember the story of Alfred burning the biscuits. Those using *Trial and Triumph* will be reading about Alfred later this term.

This is the first time we hear **King Louis IV** named, but he will not appear in person until **Chapter Five**.

King Harald the fair-haired (Harald Fairhair, *Haraldr Hárfagri*) is also mentioned. Do you know who he was? You have read stories about him in *Viking Tales*.

Reading

Part One

It would take too long to tell all the friendly and courteous words that were spoken, the greeting of the Duke and the noble old Lady Astrida, and the reception of the Barons who had come **in the train** of their Lord. Richard was **bidden** to greet them, but, though he held out his hand as desired, he shrank a little to his father's side, gazing at them in dread and shyness.

There was **Count Bernard, of Harcourt**, called the "Dane," with his shaggy red hair and beard, to which a touch of grey had given a strange unnatural tint, his eyes looking fierce and wild under his thick eyebrows, one of them mis-shapen in consequence of a sword cut, which had left a broad red and purple scar across both cheek and forehead. There, too, came tall **Baron Rainulf, of Ferrières**, cased in a linked steel **hauberk**, that rang as he walked; and the men-at-arms, with helmets and shields, looking as if Sir Eric's armour that hung in the hail had come to life and was walking about.

They sat down to Fru Astrida's banquet, the old Lady at the Duke's right hand, and the Count of Harcourt on his left. Osmond carved [the meat] for the Duke, and Richard handed his cup and trencher. All through the meal, the Duke and his Lords talked earnestly of **the expedition on which they were bound** to meet **Count Arnulf of Flanders**, on a little islet in the river Somme, there to come to some agreement, by which Arnulf might make **restitution** to **Count Herluin of Montreuil**, for certain wrongs which he had done him. Some said that this would be the fittest time for requiring Arnulf to yield up some towns on his borders, to which Normandy had long laid claim, but the Duke shook his head, saying that he must seek no selfish advantage, when called to judge between others.

Richard was rather tired of their grave talk, and thought the supper very long; but at last it was over, **the Grace** was said, the boards which had served for tables were removed, and as it was still light, some of the guests went to see how their **steeds** had been bestowed, others to look at Sir Eric's horses and hounds, and others collected together in groups.

Part Two

The Duke had time to attend to his little boy, and Richard sat upon his knee and talked, told about all his pleasures, how his arrow had hit the deer today, how Sir Eric let him ride out to the chase on his little pony, how Osmond would take him to bathe in the cool bright river, and how he had watched the raven's nest in the top of the old tower.

Duke William listened, and smiled, and seemed as well pleased to hear as the boy was to tell. "And, Richard," said he at last, "have you nought to tell me of **Father Lucas**, and his great book? What, not a word? Look up, Richard, and tell me how it goes with the learning."

"Oh, father!" said Richard, in a low voice, playing with the clasp of his father's belt, and looking down, "I don't like those crabbed letters on the old yellow **parchment**."

"But you try to learn them, I hope!" said the Duke.

"Yes, father, I do, but they are very hard, and the words are so long, and Father Lucas will always come when the sun is so bright, and the wood so green, that I know not how to bear to be kept poring over those black hooks and strokes."

"Poor little fellow," said Duke William, smiling and Richard, rather encouraged, went on more boldly. "You do not know this reading, noble father?"

"To my sorrow, no," said the Duke.

"And Sir Eric cannot read, nor Osmond, nor any one, and why must I read, and cramp my fingers with writing, just as if I was a **clerk**, instead of a young Duke?" Richard looked up in his father's face, and then hung his head, as if half-ashamed of questioning his will, but the Duke answered him without displeasure.

"It is hard, no doubt, my boy, to you now, but it will be the better for you in the end. I would give much to be able myself to read those holy books which I must now only hear read to me by a clerk, but since I have had the wish, I have had no time to learn as you have now."

"But Knights and Nobles never learn," said Richard.

"And do you think it a reason they never should? But you are wrong, my boy, for the Kings of France and England, the Counts of Anjou, of Provence, and Paris, yes, even **King Hako of Norway**, can all read."

"I tell you, Richard," [said his father], "when the treaty was drawn up for restoring this **King Louis** to his throne, I was ashamed to find myself one of the few crown vassals who could not write his name thereto."

"But none is so wise or so good as you, father," said Richard, proudly. "Sir Eric often says so."

"Sir Eric loves his Duke too well to see his faults," said Duke William; "but far better and wiser might I have been, had I been taught by such masters as you may be. And hark, Richard, not only can all Princes here read, but in England, **King Ethelstane** would have every

Noble taught; they study in his own palace, with his brothers, and read the good words that **King Alfred the truth-teller** put into their own tongue for them."

"I hate the English," said Richard, raising his head and looking very fierce.

"Hate them? and wherefore?"

"Because they traitorously killed the brave Sea King Ragnar! Fru Astrida sings his death-song, which he chanted when the **vipers** were gnawing him to death, and he gloried to think how his sons would bring the ravens to feast upon the Saxon. Oh! had I been his son, how I would have carried on the **feud**! How I would have laughed when I cut down the false traitors, and burnt their palaces!" Richard's eye kindled, and his words, as he spoke the old Norse language, flowed into the sort of wild verse in which the Sagas or legendary songs were composed, and which, perhaps, he was unconsciously repeating.

Duke William looked grave.

"Fru Astrida must sing you no more such Sagas," said he, "if they fill your mind with these revengeful thoughts, fit only for the worshippers of **Odin** and **Thor**. Neither Ragnar nor his sons knew better than to rejoice in this deadly vengeance, but we, who are Christians, know that it is for us to forgive."

"The English had slain their father!" said Richard, looking up with wondering dissatisfied eyes.

"Yes, Richard, and I speak not against them, for they were even as we should have been, had not **King Harald the fair-haired** driven your grandfather from Denmark. They had not been taught the truth, but to us it has been said, 'Forgive, and ye shall be forgiven.' Listen to me, my son, Christian as is this nation of ours, this duty of forgiveness is too often neglected, but let it not be so with you. Bear in mind, whenever you see the Cross marked on our banner, or carved in stone on the Churches, that it speaks of forgiveness to us; but of that pardon we shall never taste if we forgive not our enemies. Do you mark me, boy?"

Richard hesitated a little, and then said, "Yes, father, but I could never have pardoned, had I been one of Ragnar's sons."

"It may be that you will be in their case, Richard," said the Duke, "and should I fall, as it may well be I shall, in some of the **contests** that tear to pieces this unhappy Kingdom of France, then, remember what I say now. I charge you, on your duty to God and to your father, that you keep up no feud, no hatred, but rather that you should deem me best revenged, when you have with heart and hand, given the fullest proof of forgiveness to your enemy. Give me your word that you will."

"Yes, father," said Richard, with rather a subdued tone, and resting his head on his father's shoulder.

There was a silence for a little space, during which he began to revive into playfulness, to stroke the Duke's short curled beard, and play with his embroidered collar. In so doing, his fingers caught hold of a silver chain, and pulling it out with a jerk, he saw a silver key attached to it. "Oh, what is that?" he asked eagerly. "What does that key unlock?"

"My greatest treasure," replied Duke William, as he replaced the chain and key within his robe.

"Your greatest treasure, father! Is that your **coronet**?"

"You will know one day," said his father [*omission*]; and some of the Barons at that moment returning into the hall, he had no more leisure to bestow on his little son.

The next day, after morning service in the Chapel, and breakfast in the hall, the Duke again set forward on his journey, giving Richard hopes he might return **in a fortnight's time**, and obtaining from him a promise that he would be very attentive to Father Lucas, and very obedient to Sir Eric de Centeville.

Narration and Discussion

What are some things that Richard likes to do at the Castle of Bayeux? What does he not like as much?

Duke William asks Richard to make a very big and important promise. What is it? (Do you remember the vow that Harald made in *Viking Tales*? How was it different?)

The Duke says that maybe Fru Astrida should stop telling Richard the old Viking stories, if they give him the wrong kind of thoughts. Have you read stories (or watched shows) that gave you thoughts you didn't like? What did you do about it?

What do you think the silver key might open?

Chapter Two: Arnulf's Treachery (Part 1)

Introduction

When: A short time after Chapter One

Where: The Castle of Bayeux; later, a church in **Rouen**

Richard eagerly awaits the return of his father; but the barons bring bad news instead.

Vocabulary

her distaff, with its load of flax in her hand…: Fru Astrida is spinning the flax plant into linen thread

reposing: lying down, resting

remonstrated: complained

paying homage: a ceremonial bowing before someone to show loyalty

[his warrior] threw down "simple King Charles": Yonge's text says "Sigurd Bloodaxe," but this must be an error, as the story involves **Rollo**, King Charles the Simple, and one of Rollo's warriors. Charles made an agreement with Rollo: he would grant the Norsemen the lands of northern France, if they would swear allegiance to him, convert to Christianity, and help protect France against other warring Vikings. During the taking of the oath, Rollo was told to kiss the King's foot, but, being unwilling to do this himself, he ordered one of his men to do it instead. The warrior grabbed the King's foot and made him fall over backwards. (This story is included in *A Child's History of the World*, "A Pirate's *Great* Grandson," scheduled in Term 1, Week 11.)

ere: before

fiord: a narrow inlet of the sea between cliffs

amiss: wrong

I am thy liegeman and true vassal: I am your loyal servant

fealty: loyalty, faithfulness

treachery: betrayal, unfaithfulness

mantle: cloak

caitiff: a despicable, cowardly person

doffed his bonnet: took off his hat (out of respect)

knave: scoundrel, wicked person

cleave: split open

all restitution: to pay back everything he owed

paltry: not worth much

embarked: went on board

somewhat further: something more

chastise: punish or scold

his father had forbidden his denunciations of vengeance: his father had told him not to seek revenge

He hath the port of his grandfather, Duke Rollo: He carries himself in the same way

valiant: brave, courageous

invested with your ducal sword and mantle: officially be made Duke.

People, Places, Events

Rouen (Roo-awnh or Roo-annh) is a city on the **Seine River** in northwestern France. It has a great deal of history attached to it–one event there that you will read about later this year is the death of

Joan of Arc.

Earl Rollo: Richard's grandfather; see the introductory notes for **Chapter One**.

The false Fleming: Count Arnulf

Reading

Part One

One evening Fru Astrida sat in her tall chair in the chimney corner, **her distaff, with its load of flax in her hand, while she twisted and drew out the thread, and her spindle danced on the floor**. Opposite to her sat, sleeping in his chair, Sir Eric de Centeville; Osmond was on a low bench within the chimney corner, trimming and shaping with his knife some feathers of the wild goose, which were to fly in a different fashion from their former one, and serve, not to wing the flight of a harmless goose, but of a sharp arrow.

The men of the household sat ranged on benches on one side of the hall, the women on the other; a great red fire, together with an immense flickering lamp which hung from the ceiling, supplied the light; the windows were closed with wooden shutters, and the whole apartment had a cheerful appearance. Two or three large hounds were **reposing** in front of the hearth, and among them sat little Richard of Normandy, now smoothing down their broad silken ears; now tickling the large cushions of their feet with the end of one of Osmond's feathers; now fairly pulling open the eyes of one of the good-natured sleepy creatures, which only stretched its legs, and **remonstrated** with a sort of low groan, rather than a growl. The boy's eyes were, all the time, intently fixed on Dame Astrida, as if he would not lose one word of the story she was telling him; how **Earl Rollo**, his grandfather, had sailed into the mouth of the **Seine**, and how Archbishop Franco, of Rouen, had come to meet him and brought him the keys of the town, and how [no-one there] had met with harm from the brave Northmen. Then she told him of his grandfather's baptism, and how during the seven days that he wore his white baptismal robes, he had made large gifts to all the chief churches in his dukedom of Normandy.

"Oh, but tell of the **paying homage**!" said Richard; "and how **[his**

warrior] threw down "simple King Charles"! Ah! how would I have laughed to see it!"

"Nay, nay, Lord Richard," said the old lady, "I love not that tale. That was **ere** the Norman learnt courtesy, and rudeness ought rather to be forgotten than remembered, save for the sake of amending it. No, I will rather tell you of our coming to Centeville, and how dreary I thought these smooth [meadows], and broad soft gliding streams, compared with mine own father's **fiord** in Norway, shut in with the tall black rocks, and dark pines above them, and far away the snowy mountains rising into the sky. Ah! how blue the waters were in the long summer days when I sat in my father's boat in the little fiord, and–"

Dame Astrida was interrupted. A bugle note rang out at the castle gate; the dogs started to their feet, and uttered a sudden deafening bark; Osmond sprung up, exclaiming, "Hark!" and trying to silence the hounds; and Richard, running to Sir Eric, cried, "Wake, wake, Sir Eric, my father is come! Oh, haste to open the gate, and admit him."

"Peace, dogs!" said Sir Eric, slowly rising, as the blast of the horn was repeated. "Go, Osmond, with the porter, and see whether he who comes at such an hour be friend or foe. Stay you here, my Lord," he added, as Richard was running after Osmond; and the little boy obeyed, and stood still, though quivering all over with impatience.

"Tidings from the Duke, I should guess," said Fru Astrida. "It can scarce be himself at such an hour."

"Oh, it must be, dear Fru Astrida!" said Richard. "He said he would come again. Hark, there are horses' feet in the court! I am sure that is his black charger's tread! And I shall not be there to hold his stirrup! Oh! Sir Eric, let me go." Sir Eric, always a man of few words, only shook his head, and at that moment steps were heard on the stone stairs. Again Richard was about to spring forward, when Osmond returned, his face showing, at a glance, that something was **amiss**; but all that he said was, "Count Bernard of Harcourt, and Sir Rainulf de Ferrières," and he stood aside to let them pass.

Part Two

Richard stood still in the midst of the hall, disappointed. Without greeting to Sir Eric, or to any within the hall, the Count of Harcourt came forward to Richard, bent his knee before him, took his hand, and said with a broken voice [*omission*], "Richard, Duke of Normandy, **I am thy liegeman and true vassal**;" then rising from his knees while Rainulf de Ferrières went through the same form, the old man covered his face with his hands and wept aloud.

"Is it even so?" said the Baron de Centeville; and being answered by a mournful look and sigh from Ferrières, he too bent before the boy, and repeated the words, "I am thy liegeman and true vassal, and swear **fealty** to thee for my castle and barony of Centeville."

"Oh, no, no!" cried Richard, drawing back his hand in a sort of agony, feeling as if he was in a frightful dream from which he could not awake. "What means it? Oh! Fru Astrida, tell me what means it? Where is my father?"

"Alas, my child!" said the old lady, putting her arm round him, and drawing him close to her, whilst her tears flowed fast, and Richard stood, reassured by her embrace, listening with eyes open wide, and deep oppressed breathing, to what was passing between the four nobles, who spoke earnestly among themselves, without much heed of him.

"The Duke dead!" repeated Sir Eric de Centeville, like one stunned and stupefied.

"Even so," said Rainulf, slowly and sadly, and the silence was only broken by the long-drawn sobs of old Count Bernard.

"But how? when? where?" broke forth Sir Eric, presently. "There was no note of battle when you went forth. Oh, why was not I at his side?"

"He fell not in battle," gloomily replied Sir Rainulf.

"Ha! could sickness cut him down so quickly?"

"It was not sickness," answered Ferrières. "It was **treachery**. He fell in the Isle of Pecquigny, by the hand of **the false Fleming**!"

"Lives the traitor yet?" cried the Baron de Centeville, grasping his good sword.

"He lives and rejoices in his crime," said Ferrières, "safe in his own merchant towns."

"I can scarce credit you, my Lords!" said Sir Eric. "Our Duke slain, and his enemy safe, and you here to tell the tale!"

"I would I were stark and stiff by my Lord's side!" said Count Bernard, "but for the sake of Normandy, and of that poor child, who is like to need all that ever were friends to his house. I would that mine eyes had been blinded for ever, ere they had seen that sight! And not a sword lifted in his defence! Tell you how it passed, Rainulf! My tongue will not speak it!"

He threw himself on a bench and covered his face with his **mantle**, while Rainulf de Ferrières proceeded: "You know how in an evil hour our good Duke appointed to meet this **caitiff**, Count of Flanders, in the Isle of Pecquigny, the Duke and Count each bringing twelve men with them, all unarmed. Duke Alan of Brittany was one on our side, Count Bernard here another, old Count Bothon and myself; we bore no weapon–would that we had–but not so the false Flemings. Ah me! I shall never forget Duke William's lordly presence when he stepped ashore, and **doffed his bonnet** to the **knave** Arnulf."

"Yes," interposed Bernard. "And marked you not the words of the traitor, as they met? 'My Lord,' quoth he, 'you are my shield and defence.' Would that I could **cleave** his treason-hatching skull with my battle-axe."

"So," continued Rainulf, "they conferred together, and as words cost nothing to Arnulf, he not only promised **all restitution** to the **paltry** Montreuil, but even was for offering to pay homage to our Duke for Flanders itself; but this our William refused, saying it were foul wrong to both King Louis of France and Kaiser Otho of Germany, to take from them their vassal. They took leave of each other in all courtesy, and we **embarked** again. It was Duke William's pleasure to go alone in a small boat, while we twelve were together in another. Just as we had nearly reached our own bank, there was a shout from the Flemings that their Count had **somewhat further** to say to the Duke, and forbidding us to follow him, the Duke turned his boat and went back again. No sooner had he set foot on the isle," proceeded the Norman, clenching his hands, and speaking between his teeth, "than we saw one Fleming strike him on the head with an oar; he fell senseless, the rest threw themselves upon him, and the next moment held up their bloody daggers in scorn at us! You may well think how we shouted and yelled at them, and plied our oars like men distracted, but all in vain, they were already in their boats, and ere we could even reach the isle, they were on the other side of the river, mounted their horses, fled with coward speed, and were out of reach of a Norman's vengeance."

Part Three

"But they shall not be so long!" cried Richard, starting forward; for to his childish fancy this dreadful history was more like one of Dame Astrida's legends than a reality, and at the moment his thought was only of the blackness of the treason. "Oh, that I were a man to **chastise** them! One day they shall feel–"

He broke off short, for he remembered how **his father had forbidden his denunciations of vengeance**, but his words were eagerly caught up by the Barons, who, as Duke William had said, were far from possessing any temper of forgiveness, thought revenge a duty, and were only glad to see a warlike spirit in their new Prince.

"Ha! say you so, my young Lord?" exclaimed old Count Bernard, rising. "Yes, and I see a sparkle in your eye that tells me you will one day avenge him nobly!"

Richard drew up his head, and his heart throbbed high as Sir Eric made answer, "Aye, truly, that will he! You might search Normandy through, yea, and Norway likewise, ere you would find a temper more bold and free. Trust my word, Count Bernard, our young Duke will be famed as widely as ever were his forefathers!"

"I believe it well!" said Bernard. "**He hath the port of his grandfather, Duke Rollo**, and much, too, of his noble father! How say you, Lord Richard, will you be a **valiant** leader of the Norman race against our foes?"

"That I will!" said Richard, carried away by the applause excited by those few words of his. "I will ride at your head this very night if you will but go to chastise the false Flemings."

"You shall ride with us tomorrow, my Lord," answered Bernard, "but it must be to Rouen, there to be **invested with your ducal sword and mantle**, and to receive the homage of your vassals."

Part Four

Richard drooped his head without replying, for this seemed to bring to him the perception that his father was really gone, and that he should never see him again. He thought of all his projects for the day of his return, how he had almost counted the hours, and had looked forward to telling him that Father Lucas was well pleased with him!

And now he should never nestle into his breast again, never hear his voice, never see those kind eyes beam upon him. Large tears gathered in his eyes, and ashamed that they should be seen, he sat down on a footstool at Fru Astrida's feet, leant his forehead on his hands, and thought over all that his father had done and said the last time they were together. He fancied the return that had been promised, going over the meeting and the greeting, till he had almost persuaded himself that this dreadful story was but a dream.

But when he looked up, there were the Barons, with their grave mournful faces, speaking of the corpse, which Duke Alan of Brittany was escorting to Rouen, there to be buried beside the old Duke Rollo, and the Duchess Emma, Richard's mother. Then he lost himself in wonder how that stiff bleeding body could be the same as the father whose arm was so lately around him, and whether his father's spirit knew how he was thinking of him; and in these dreamy thoughts, the young orphan Duke of Normandy, forgotten by his vassals in their grave councils, fell asleep, and scarce wakened enough to attend to his prayers, when Fru Astrida at length remembered him, and led him away to bed.

Narration and Discussion

It is just as hard for Richard to understand that he is now the Duke of Normandy, as it is to make sense of the fact that his father is dead. How do you think his life might change because of these things?

Richard says, "Oh, that I were a man to chastise [punish] them! One day they shall feel–" How do the Barons react to this? What might Richard's father say?

For further thought: People are already asking Richard to do some very big and hard things. What is the hardest thing you have ever been asked to do? Were you able to do it?

Creative narration: This scene is a sad one, but some children might enjoy acting it out. An alternative would be to dictate a letter about it, taking the part of one of the characters; or to have someone act as a news reporter, telling what has happened and what the next plans are.

Chapter Two: Arnulf's Treachery (Part 2)

Introduction

When Richard is taken to view the body of his father, his first impulse (again) is to vow revenge on the murderers; but this time he is interrupted by someone with different ideas.

Vocabulary

grave: solemn, serious

inferior: lower, less

largesses: generosity

moat: a ditch surrounding a castle or fort, or even (in this case) a city; usually filled with water to keep enemies out

the deceased: the one who has died; the body

bier: platform

oppression on his breast: feeling of tightness in his chest

ermine: a kind of fur

hair shirt: a rough garment worn by monks that would irritate the skin; worn as a sign of humility and to share in Christ's suffering

abye it: pay the penalty for it

hilt: handle

countenance: face

pledged: promised, sworn

washed in yonder blessed font: baptized in this church, in that baptismal font

assent: agreement

if thou dost vow aught: if you vow anything

People, Places, Events

Church of Our Lady (*Cathédrale primatiale Notre-Dame de l'Assomption de Rouen*), better known as **Rouen Cathedral:** A church with a long history that would make a book in itself. The building went through a number of restoration projects, each one in whatever architectural style was popular at the time; so it ended up with three towers, each in a different style. In 1822 (shortly before *The Little Duke* was written), the spire of the central tower was struck by lightning, and it was replaced by a new iron spire, which made the church (for a time) the tallest building in the world. (That spire itself caught fire in July 2024.) If you want to see what similar churches looked like in Richard's time, an online image search for "Norman church" will bring up some good examples.

Martin, Abbot of Jumièges: An Abbot is the head of a monastery.

Jumièges: A village about 13 miles (21 km) west of Rouen, and the site of **Jumièges Abbey**, which had been destroyed by Vikings but (as we hear later from Abbot Martin) was rebuilt by Duke William.

Reading

Part One

When Richard awoke the next morning, he could hardly believe that all that had passed in the evening was true, but soon he found that it was but too real, and all was prepared for him to go to Rouen with the vassals; indeed, it was for no other purpose than to fetch him that the Count of Harcourt had come to Bayeux. Fru Astrida was quite unhappy that "the child," as she called him, should go alone with the warriors; but Sir Eric laughed at her, and said that it would never do for the Duke of Normandy to bring his nurse with him in his first entry into Rouen, and she must be content to follow at some space behind under the escort of Walter the huntsman.

So she took leave of Richard, charging both Sir Eric and Osmond to have the utmost care of him, and shedding tears as if the parting was to be for a much longer space; then he bade farewell to the servants of the castle, received the blessing of Father Lucas, and mounting his pony, rode off between Sir Eric and Count Bernard.

Richard was but a little boy, and he did not think so much of his loss, as he rode along in the free morning air, feeling himself a Prince at the head of his vassals, his banner displayed before him, and the people coming out wherever he passed to gaze on him, and call for blessings on his name. Rainulf de Ferrières carried a large heavy purse filled with silver and gold, and whenever they came to these gazing crowds, Richard was well pleased to thrust his hands deep into it, and scatter handfuls of coins among the gazers, especially where he saw little children.

They stopped to dine and rest in the middle of the day, at the castle of a Baron, who, as soon as the meal was over, mounted his horse, and joined them in their ride to Rouen. So far it had not been very different from Richard's last journey, when he went to keep Christmas there with his father; but now they were beginning to come nearer the town, he knew the broad river Seine again, and saw the square tower of the Cathedral, and he remembered how at that very place his father had met him, and how he had ridden by his side into the town, and had been led by his hand up to the hall.

His heart was very heavy, as he recollected there was no one now to meet and welcome him; scarcely any one to whom he could even tell his thoughts, for those tall **grave** Barons had nothing to say to such a little boy, and the very respect and formality with which they treated him, made him shrink from them still more, especially from the grim-faced Bernard; and Osmond, his own friend and playfellow, was obliged to ride far behind, as **inferior** in rank.

Part Two

They entered the town just as it was growing dark. Count Bernard looked back and arrayed the procession; Eric de Centeville bade Richard sit upright and not look weary, and then all the Knights held back while the little Duke rode alone a little in advance of them through the gateway.

There was a loud shout of "Long live the little Duke!" and crowds of people were standing round to gaze upon his entry, so many that the bag of coins was soon emptied by his **largesses**. The whole city was like one great castle, shut in by a wall and **moat**, and with Rollo's Tower rising at one end like the keep of a castle, and it was thither that Richard was turning his horse, when the Count of Harcourt said, "Nay, my Lord, to the **Church of our Lady**."

It was then considered a duty to be paid to **the deceased**, that their relatives and friends should visit them as they lay in state, and sprinkle them with drops of holy water, and Richard was now to pay this token of respect. He trembled a little, and yet it did not seem quite so dreary, since he should once more look on his father's face, and he accordingly rode towards the Cathedral. It was then very unlike what it is now; the walls were very thick, the windows small and almost buried in heavy carved arches, the columns within were low, clumsy, and circular, and it was usually so dark that the vaulting of the roof could scarcely be seen.

Now, however, a whole flood of light poured forth from every window, and when Richard came to the door, he saw not only the two tall thick candles that always burnt on each side of the Altar, but in the Chancel stood a double row ranged in a square, shedding a pure, quiet brilliancy throughout the building, and chiefly on the silver and gold ornaments of the Altar. Outside these lights knelt a row of priests in dark garments, their heads bowed over their clasped hands, and their chanted psalms sounding sweet, and full of soothing music. Within that guarded space was a **bier**, and a form lay on it.

Richard trembled still more with awe, and would have paused, but he was obliged to proceed. He dipped his hand in the water of the font, crossed his brow, and came slowly on, sprinkled the remaining drops on the lifeless figure, and then stood still. There was an **oppression on his breast** as if he could neither breathe nor move.

Part Three

There lay William of the Long Sword, like a good and true Christian warrior, arrayed in his shining armour, his sword by his side, his shield on his arm, and a cross between his hands, clasped upon his breast.

His ducal mantle of crimson velvet, lined with **ermine**, was round his shoulders, and, instead of a helmet, his coronet was on his head; but, in contrast with this rich array, over the collar of the hauberk, was folded the edge of a rough **hair shirt**, which the Duke had worn beneath his robes, unknown to all, until his corpse was disrobed of his blood-stained garments. His face looked full of calm, solemn peace, as if he had gently fallen asleep, and was only awaiting the great call to awaken.

There was not a single token of violence visible about him, save that one side of his forehead bore a deep purple mark, where he had first been struck by the blow of the oar which had deprived him of sense.

"See you that, my Lord?" said Count Bernard, first breaking the silence, in a low, deep, stern voice.

Richard had heard little for many hours past [but] counsels against the Flemings, and plans of bitter enmity against them; and the sight of his murdered father, with that look and tone of the old Dane, fired his spirit, and breaking from his trance of silent awe and grief, he exclaimed, "I see it, and dearly shall the traitor Fleming **abye it**!" Then, encouraged by the applauding looks of the nobles, he proceeded, feeling like one of the young champions of Fru Astrida's songs. His cheek was coloured, his eye lighted up, and he lifted his head, so that the hair fell back from his forehead; he laid his hand on the **hilt** of his father's sword, and spoke on in words, perhaps, suggested by some sage. "Yes, Arnulf of Flanders, know that Duke William of Normandy shall not rest unavenged! On this good sword I vow, that, as soon as my arm shall have strength–"

The rest was left unspoken, for a hand was laid on his arm. A priest, who had hitherto been kneeling near the head of the corpse, had risen, and stood tall and dark over him, and, looking up, he recognized the pale, grave **countenance** of **Martin, Abbot of Jumièges**, his father's chief friend and councillor.

"Richard of Normandy, what sayest thou?" said he, sternly. "Yes, hang thy head, and reply not, rather than repeat those words. Dost thou come here to disturb the peace of the dead with clamours for vengeance? Dost thou vow strife and anger on that sword which was never drawn, save in the cause of the poor and distressed? Wouldst thou rob Him, to whose service thy life has been **pledged**, and devote thyself to that of His foe? Is this what thou hast learnt from thy blessed father?"

Richard made no answer, but he covered his face with his hands, to hide the tears which were fast streaming.

"Lord Abbot, Lord Abbot, this passes!" exclaimed Bernard the Dane. "Our young Lord is no monk, and we will not see each spark of noble and knightly spirit quenched as soon as it shows itself."

"Count of Harcourt," said Abbot Martin, "are these the words of a savage Pagan, or of one who has been **washed in yonder blessed font**? Never, while I have power, shalt thou darken the child's soul with thy foul thirst of revenge, insult the presence of thy master with the crime he so abhorred, nor the temple of Him who came to pardon, with thy hatred. Well do I know, ye Barons of Normandy, that each drop of your blood would willingly be given, could it bring back our departed Duke, or guard his orphan child; but, if ye have loved the father, do his bidding–lay aside that accursed spirit of hatred and vengeance; if ye love the child, seek not to injure his soul more deeply than even his bitterest foe, were it Arnulf himself, hath power to hurt him."

The Barons were silenced, whatever their thoughts might be, and Abbot Martin turned to Richard, whose tears were still dropping fast through his fingers, as the thought of those last words of his father returned more clearly upon him. The Abbot laid his hand on his head, and spoke gently to him. "These are tears of a softened heart, I trust," said he. "I well believe that thou didst scarce know what thou wert saying."

"Forgive me!" said Richard, as well as he could speak.

"See there," said the priest, pointing to the large Cross over the Altar, "thou knowest the meaning of that sacred sign?"

Richard bowed his head in **assent** and reverence.

"It speaks of forgiveness," continued the Abbot. "And knowest thou who gave that pardon? The Son forgave His murderers; the Father them who slew His Son. And shalt thou call for vengeance?"

"But oh!" said Richard, looking up, "must that cruel, murderous traitor glory unpunished in his crime, while there lies–" and again his voice was cut off by tears.

"Vengeance shall surely overtake the sinner," said Martin, "the vengeance of the Lord, and in His own good time, but it must not be of thy seeking. Nay, Richard, thou art of all men the most bound to show love and mercy to Arnulf of Flanders. Yes, when the hand of the Lord hath touched him, and bowed him down in punishment for his crime, it is then, that thou, whom he hath most deeply injured, shouldst stretch out thine hand to aid him, and receive him with pardon and peace. **If thou dost vow aught** on the sword of thy blessed father, in the sanctuary of thy Redeemer, let it be a Christian vow."

Richard wept too bitterly to speak, and Bernard de Harcourt, taking his hand, led him away from the Church.

Narration and Discussion

Why does Richard find the different ideas of the adults in his life so confusing? Who does he most want to please? Do you think he will ever have to put these beliefs to the test?

Can you think of any other stories where someone had to choose between paying back evil for evil, and forgiveness? Here's one:

> 4 And Joseph said unto his brethren, Come near to me, I pray you. And they came near. And he said, I am Joseph your brother, whom ye sold into Egypt.
>
> 5 Now therefore be not grieved, nor angry with yourselves, that ye sold me hither: for God did send me before you to preserve life. (Genesis 45:4-5)

Chapter Three: Duke William's Treasure (Part 1)

Introduction

When: The next day

Where: The Cathedral of Rouen; later, Duke William's castle

Duke William is buried, and Richard is crowned as the new Duke. How will he manage such a task? Who can he trust to help him?

In Other News

If you are following the AO reading schedule, this week you will be reading about the Norse explorer Leif Erikson (his first name can be spelled Lief, and spellings of his last name also vary). Leif is believed to have been born (probably in Iceland) in the 970's–which would put him a generation or two after Duke Richard.

Vocabulary

in high pomp and state: with much ceremony

as he was desired: as he was asked to do

ranks: The nobles lined up according to their **rank** or **ranks** means that the important and wealthy ones came first, followed by the rest. The **clergy ranged in ranks** could refer to important priests having special places in the church, but more likely just means that they were sitting or standing in rows.

clergy: priests

mitres: pointed caps

pastoral staff: ceremonial rod

***Te Deum Laudamus*:** "We praise you, God"

the Choir: a part of the church

Confirmation: a rite of the church confirming one's baptism. Because Richard had already been confirmed, he was allowed to receive **Holy Communion** (eat the bread and drink the wine).

iniquity: sin, wrongdoing

awful: solemn, awesome

oath: solemn promise or agreement

girded: belted, attached

People, Places, Events

The Archbishop of Rouen: the priest in charge of the Cathedral

Alberic de Montémar: a young noble only a few years older than Richard, from **Montémar sur Epte**. We are told in a later chapter that his father had fought with Duke William, and was killed "by your father's side…at the time when you were born, Lord Richard." There was a battle at the time of Richard's birth; and the **Epte** river was and still is the boundary between Normandy and the rest of France; but both Alberic and the castle of Montémar seem to be imagined for this story.

Reading

Part One

Duke William of the Long Sword was buried the next morning **in high pomp and state**, with many a prayer and psalm chanted over his grave.

When this was over, little Richard, who had all the time stood or knelt nearest the corpse, in one dull heavy dream of wonder and sorrow, was led back to the palace, and there his long, heavy, black garments were taken off, and he was dressed in his short scarlet tunic, his hair was carefully arranged, and then he came down again into the hall, where there was a great assembly of Barons, some in armour, some in long furred gowns, who had all been attending his father's burial. Richard, **as he was desired** by Sir Eric de Centeville, took off his cap, and bowed low in reply to the reverences with which they all greeted his entrance, and he then slowly crossed the hall, and descended the steps from the door, while they formed into a procession behind him, according to their **ranks**–the Duke of Brittany first, and then all the rest, down to the poorest knight [*omission*].

Thus, they proceeded, in slow and solemn order, till they came to the church of our Lady. The **clergy** were there already, **ranged in ranks** on each side of the Choir; and the Bishops, in their **mitres** and rich robes, each with his **pastoral staff** in his hand, were standing round the Altar. As the little Duke entered, there arose from all the voices in the Chancel the full, loud, clear chant of ***Te Deum***

Laudamus, echoing among the dark vaults of the roof. To that sound, Richard walked up **the Choir**, to a large, heavy, crossed-legged, carved chair, raised on two steps, just before the steps of the Altar began, and there he stood, Bernard de Harcourt and Eric de Centeville on each side of him, and all his other vassals in due order, in the Choir.

After the beautiful chant of the hymn was ended, the service for the **Holy Communion** began. When the time came for the offering, each noble gave gold or silver; and, lastly, Rainulf of Ferrières came up to the step of the Altar with a cushion, on which was placed a circlet of gold, the ducal coronet; and another Baron, following him closely, carried a long, heavy sword, with a cross handle. The Archbishop of Rouen received both coronet and sword, and laid them on the Altar. Then the service proceeded. At that time the rite of **Confirmation** was administered in infancy, and Richard, who had been confirmed by his godfather, the Archbishop of Rouen, immediately after his baptism, knelt in solemn awe to receive the other Holy Sacrament from his hands, as soon as all the clergy had [done so].

Part Two

When [that] was over, Richard was led forward to the step of the Altar by Count Bernard, and Sir Eric, and the Archbishop, laying one hand upon both his, as he held them clasped together, demanded of him, in the name of God, and of the people of Normandy, whether he would be their good and true ruler, guard them from their foes, maintain truth, punish **iniquity**, and protect the Church.

"I will!" answered Richard's young, trembling voice, "So help me God!" and he knelt, and kissed the book of the Holy Gospels, which the Archbishop offered him.

It was a great and **awful oath**, and he dreaded to think that he had taken it. He still knelt, put both hands over his face, and whispered, "O God, my Father, help me to keep it."

The Archbishop waited till he rose, and then, turning him with his face to the people, said, "Richard, by the grace of God, I invest thee with the ducal mantle of Normandy!"

Two of the Bishops then hung round his shoulders a crimson velvet mantle, furred with ermine, which, made as it was for a grown man, hung heavily on the poor child's shoulders, and lay in heaps on the ground. The Archbishop then set the golden coronet on his long, flowing hair, where it hung so loosely on the little head, that Sir Eric was obliged to put his hand to it to hold it safe; and, lastly, the long, straight, two-handed sword was brought and placed in his hand, with another solemn bidding to use it ever in maintaining the right. It should have been **girded** to his side, but the great sword was so much taller than the little Duke, that, as it stood upright by him, he was obliged to raise his arm to put it round the handle.

He then had to return to his throne, which was not done without some difficulty, encumbered as he was, but Osmond held up the train of his mantle, Sir Eric kept the coronet on his head, and he himself held fast and lovingly the sword, though the Count of Harcourt offered to carry it for him. He was lifted up to his throne, and then came the paying him homage; Alan, Duke of Brittany, was the first to kneel before him, and with his hand between those of the Duke, he swore to be his man, to obey him, and pay him feudal service for his dukedom of Brittany. In return, Richard swore to be his good Lord, and to protect him from all his foes.

Then followed Bernard the Dane, and many another, each repeating the same formulary, as their large rugged hands were clasped within those little soft fingers. Many a kind and loving eye was bent in compassion on the orphan child; many a strong voice faltered with earnestness as it pronounced the vow, and many a brave, stalwart heart heaved with grief for the murdered father, and tears flowed down the war-worn cheeks which had met the fiercest storms of the northern ocean, as they bent before the young fatherless boy, whom they loved for the sake of his conquering grandfather, and his brave and pious father. Few Normans were there whose hearts did not glow at the touch of those small hands, with a love almost of a parent, for their young Duke.

Part Three

The ceremony of receiving homage lasted long and Richard, though interested and touched at first, grew very weary; the crown and mantle were so heavy, the faces succeeded each other like figures in an endless dream, and the constant repetition of the same words was very tedious. He grew sleepy, he longed to jump up, to lean to the right or left, or to speak something besides that regular form. He gave one great yawn, but it brought him such a frown from the stern face of Bernard, as quite to wake him for a few minutes, and make him sit upright, and receive the next vassal with as much attention as he had shown the first, but he looked imploringly at Sir Eric, as if to ask if it ever would be over.

At last, far down among the Barons, came one at whose sight Richard revived a little. It was a boy only a few years older than himself, perhaps about ten, with a pleasant brown face, black hair, and quick black eyes which glanced, with a look between friendliness and respect, up into the little Duke's gazing face. Richard listened eagerly for his name, and was refreshed at the sound of the boyish voice which pronounced, "I, Alberic de Montémar, am thy liegeman and vassal for my castle and barony of **Montémar sur Epte**."

When Alberic moved away, Richard followed him with his eye as far as he could to his place in the Cathedral, and was taken by surprise when he found the next Baron kneeling before him.

Narration and Discussion

During the service, it is noted that the coronet almost falls off Richard's head; the velvet mantle "hung heavily on the poor child's shoulders, and lay in heaps on the ground"; and the sword Richard is given is taller than he is. Why do you think the author keeps repeating the point about everything being too big for Richard?

What are the things Richard swore he would do as Duke? Do you think it was a good idea to ask God to help him keep this vow?

Creative narration: If there are two or more students, act out the part of two nobles, perhaps sitting in the back row and chatting during the long service. An alternative if there is just one: take the part of young Alberic, and tell what he might be thinking about all this.

Chapter Three: Duke William's Treasure (Part 2)

Introduction

When: That evening

Where: The Duke's castle in Rouen

In this chapter we find out what Duke William considered his greatest treasure.

Vocabulary

would fain have: would have liked to

toils: chores

your colour mantles: you are embarrassed

liegemen: underlings, vassals

forbearance: patience

recreant: unfaithful; can also mean cowardly

coffers: money chests

rude: plain, rough

serge: heavy wool

wretched fare: terrible food

wild boar: wild pig

endowed it richly: donated money for its support

temporal affairs: earthly business

receive his vows: accept him as a monk

turmoil: confusion and noise

"saw a white cap at a doorway": saw Fru Astrida

People, Places, Events

Frank: one of the tribe of the Franks; referring to King Louis of France

Sea-King, Hasting: Also called **Hastein** or **Haesteinn of Nantes**; the Viking who was responsible for destroying the Abbey of Jumièges.

Reading

Part One

The ceremony of homage came to an end at last, and Richard **would fain have** run all the way to the palace to shake off his weariness, but he was obliged to head the procession again; and even when he reached the castle hall his **toils** were not over, for there was a great state banquet spread out, and he had to sit in the high chair where he remembered climbing on his father's knee last Christmas-day, all the time that the Barons feasted round, and held grave converse. Richard's best comfort all this time was in watching Osmond de Centeville and Alberic de Montémar, who, with the other youths who were not yet knighted, were waiting on those who sat at the table. At last he grew so very weary, that he fell fast asleep in the corner of his chair, and did not wake till he was startled by the rough voice of Bernard de Harcourt, calling him to rouse up, and bid the Duke of Brittany farewell.

"Poor child!" said Duke Alan, as Richard rose up, startled, "he is over-wearied with this day's work. Take care of him, Count Bernard; thou art a kindly nurse, but a rough one for such a babe. Ha! my young Lord, **your colour mantles** at being called a babe! I crave your pardon, for you are a fine spirit. And hark you, Lord Richard of Normandy, I have little cause to love your race, and little right, I trow, had King Charles the Simple to call us free Bretons **liegemen** to a race of plundering Northern pirates. To Duke Rollo's might, my father never gave his homage; nay, nor did I yield it for all Duke William's long sword, but I did pay it to his **generosity** and **forbearance**, and now I grant it to thy weakness and to his noble memory. I doubt not that the **recreant** Frank, Louis, whom he restored to his throne, will strive to profit by thy youth and helplessness, and should that be, remember that thou hast no surer friend than Alan of Brittany. Fare thee well, my young Duke."

"Farewell, Sir," said Richard, willingly giving his hand to be shaken by his kind vassal, and watching him as Sir Eric attended him from the hall.

"Fair words, but I trust not the Breton," muttered Bernard; "hatred is deeply ingrained in them."

"He should know what the **Frank** King is made of," said Rainulf de Ferrières; "he was bred up with him in the days that they were both exiles at the court of King Ethelstane of England."

"Aye, and thanks to Duke William that either Louis or Alan are not exiles still. Now we shall see whose gratitude is worth most, the Frank's or the Breton's. I suspect the Norman valour will be the best to trust to."

"Yes, and how will Norman valour prosper without treasure? Who knows what gold is in the Duke's **coffers**?"

There was some consultation here in a low voice, and the next thing Richard heard distinctly was, that one of the Nobles held up a silver chain and key, saying that they had been found on the Duke's neck, and that he had kept them, thinking that they doubtless led to something of importance.

"Oh, yes!" said Richard, eagerly, "I know it. He told me it was the key to his greatest treasure."

Part Two

The Normans heard this with great interest, and it was resolved that several of the most trusted persons, among whom were the Archbishop of Rouen, Abbot Martin of Jumièges, and the Count of Harcourt, should go immediately in search of this precious hoard. Richard accompanied them up the narrow rough stone stairs, to the large dark apartment, where his father had slept. Though a Prince's chamber, it had little furniture; a low uncurtained bed, a Cross on a ledge near its head, a **rude** table, a few chairs, and two large chests, were all it contained. Harcourt tried the lid of one of the chests: it opened, and proved to be full of wearing apparel; he went to the other, which was smaller, much more carved, and ornamented with very handsome iron-work. It was locked, and putting in the key, it fitted, the lock turned, and the chest was opened. The Normans pressed eagerly to see their Duke's greatest treasure.

It was a robe of **serge**, and a pair of sandals, such as were worn in the Abbey of Jumièges.

"Ha! is this all? What didst say, child?" cried Bernard the Dane, hastily.

"He told me it was his greatest treasure!" repeated Richard.

"And it was!" said Abbot Martin.

Part Three

Then the good Abbot told them the history, part of which was already known to some of them. About five or six years before, Duke William had been hunting in the forest of Jumièges, when he had suddenly come on the ruins of the Abbey, which had been wasted thirty or forty years previously by the **Sea-King, Hasting**. Two old monks, of the original brotherhood, still survived, and came forth to greet the Duke, and offer him their hospitality.

"Ay!" said Bernard, "well do I remember their bread; we asked if it was made of fir-bark, like that of our brethren of Norway."

William, then an eager, thoughtless young man, turned with disgust from this **wretched fare**, and throwing the old men some gold, galloped on to enjoy his hunting. In the course of the sport, he was left alone, and encountered a **wild boar**, which threw him down, trampled on him, and left him stretched senseless on the ground, severely injured. His companions coming up, carried him, as the nearest place of shelter, to the ruins of Jumièges, where the two old monks gladly received him in the remaining portion of their house. As soon as he recovered his senses, he earnestly asked their pardon for his pride, and the scorn he had shown to the poverty and patient suffering which he should have reverenced.

William had always been a man who chose the good and refused the evil, but this accident, and the long illness that followed it, made him far more thoughtful and serious than he had ever been before. He made preparing for death and eternity his first object, and thought less of his worldly affairs, his wars, and his ducal state. He rebuilt the old Abbey, **endowed it richly**, and sent for Martin himself from France, to become the Abbot; he delighted in nothing so much as praying there, conversing with the Abbot, and hearing him read holy books; and he felt his **temporal affairs**, and the state and splendour of his rank, so great a temptation, that he had one day come to the Abbot, and entreated to be allowed to lay them aside, and become a brother of the order. But Martin had refused to **receive his vows**. He had told him that he had no right to neglect or forsake the duties of the station which God had appointed him; that it would be a sin to leave the post which had been given him to defend; and that the way marked out for him to serve God was by doing justice among his people, and using his power to defend the right. Not till he had done his allotted work, and his son was old enough to take his place as ruler of the Normans, might he cease from his active duties, quit the **turmoil** of the world, and seek the repose of the cloister. It was in this hope of peaceful retirement, that William had delighted to treasure up the humble garments that he hoped one day to wear in peace and holiness.

"And oh! my noble Duke!" exclaimed Abbot Martin, bursting into tears, as he finished his narration, "the Lord hath been very gracious unto thee! He has taken thee home to thy rest, long before thou didst dare to hope for it."

Slowly, and with subdued feelings, the Norman Barons left the chamber; Richard, whom they seemed to have almost forgotten, wandered to the stairs, to find his way to the room where he had slept last night. He had not made many steps before he heard Osmond's voice say, "Here, my Lord"; he looked up, **saw a white cap at a doorway** a little above him, he bounded up and flew into Dame Astrida's outstretched arms.

How glad he was to sit in her lap, and lay his wearied head on her bosom, while, with a worn-out voice, he exclaimed, "Oh, Fru Astrida! I am very, very tired of being Duke of Normandy!"

Narration and Discussion

Why were the contents of the locked trunk so surprising? How did the Norman Barons react?

Why did Abbot Martin refuse to let Duke William become a monk?

For further exploration: "…he had to sit in the high chair where he remembered climbing on his father's knee last Christmas-day…" The mention of Christmas here may get lost in the swarm of other events. However, it is a reminder that the Normans, like other Christians in the Middle Ages, celebrated many of the same holy days we do today. What can you find out about how Christmas might have looked, sounded, or tasted in a castle, around the year 950 or 1000 A.D.? A website called Castles and Turrets has an interesting article called "Medieval Festivities: What was Christmas like During this Time?"

Chapter Four: In the Hands of the Frank (Part 1)

Introduction

When: Shortly after the funeral and investiture ceremonies

Where: Rouen

Richard makes friends with Alberic, the young Baron de Montémar, who came to Rouen for the ceremonies.

In Other News

If you are following the AO reading schedule, this week you will be reading about "Real Castles" in Hillyer's *A Child's History of the World* (which contains some useful vocabulary); or "The Hardy Northmen" in Synge's *Discovery of New Worlds*. "The Hardy Northmen" gives background on the Vikings, and tells the story of Richard's grandfather Rollo.

Vocabulary

warden: keeper, protector

marches: border areas

Seneschal or **Steward:** a manager of the household, one of the head servants

flaxen: blond

the gigantic stature of his grandfather, Earl Rollo: Rollo was apparently so large that he could not find a horse big and strong enough to carry him; and that is how he came by his nickname "The Walker."

exploit: daring trick

battlements: a low wall with open spaces to shoot through

being giddy: feeling dizzy

precipices: cliffs

bred up with my Lord Duke: raised with him

People, Places, Events

Dame de Centeville: French way of saying "Lady Centeville"

Reading

Part One

Richard of Normandy was very anxious to know more of the little boy whom he had seen among his vassals.

"Ah! the young Baron de Montémar," said Sir Eric. "I knew his father well, and a brave man he was, though not of northern blood. He was **warden** of the **marches** of the Epte, and was killed by your father's side [during an uprising], at the time when you were born, Lord Richard."

"But where does he live? Shall I not see him again?"

"Montémar is on the bank of the Epte, in the domain that the French wrongfully claim from us. He lives there with his mother, and if he be not yet returned, you shall see him presently. Osmond, go you and seek out the lodgings of the young Montémar, and tell him the Duke would see him."

Richard had never had a playfellow of his own age, and his eagerness to see Alberic de Montémar was great. He watched from the window, and at length beheld Osmond entering the court with a boy of ten years old by his side, and an old grey-headed Squire, with a golden chain to mark him as a **Seneschal** or **Steward** of the Castle, walking behind.

Richard ran to the door to meet them, holding out his hand eagerly. Alberic uncovered his bright dark hair, bowed low and gracefully, but stood as if he did not exactly know what to do next. Richard grew shy at the same moment, and the two boys stood looking at each other somewhat awkwardly. It was easy to see that they were of different races, so unlike were the blue eyes, **flaxen** hair, and fair face of the young Duke, to the black flashing eyes and olive cheek of his French vassal, who, though two years older, was scarcely above him in height; and his slight figure, well-proportioned, active and agile as it was, did not give the same promise of strength as the round limbs and large-boned frame of Richard, which even now seemed likely to rival **the gigantic stature of his grandfather, Earl Rollo, [the Walker]**.

For some minutes the little Duke and the young Baron stood surveying each other without a word, and old Sir Eric did not improve matters by saying, "Well, Lord Duke, here he is. Have you no better greeting for him?"

"The children are shame-faced," said Fru Astrida, seeing how they both coloured. "Is your Lady mother in good health, my young sir?"

Alberic blushed more deeply, bowed to the old northern lady, and answered fast and low in French, "I cannot speak the Norman tongue."

Richard, glad to say something, interpreted Fru Astrida's speech, and Alberic readily made courteous reply that his mother was well, and he thanked the **Dame de Centeville**, a French title which sounded new to Fru Astrida's ears. Then came the embarrassment again, and Fru Astrida at last said, "Take him out, Lord Richard; take him to see the horses in the stables, or the hounds, or what not."

Richard was not sorry to obey, so out they went into the court of Rollo's tower, and in the open air the shyness went off. Richard showed his own pony, and Alberic asked if he could leap into the saddle without putting his foot in the stirrup. No, Richard could not; indeed, even Osmond had never seen it done, for the feats of French chivalry had scarcely yet spread into Normandy.

"Can you?" said Richard; "will you show us?"

"I know I can with my own pony," said Alberic, "for Bertrand will not let me mount in any other way; but I will try with yours, if you desire it, my Lord."

So the pony was led out. Alberic laid one hand on its mane, and vaulted on its back in a moment. Both Osmond and Richard broke out loudly into admiration. "Oh, this is nothing!" said Alberic. "Bertrand says it is nothing. Before he grew old and stiff he could spring into the saddle in this manner fully armed. I ought to do this much better."

Richard begged to be shown how to perform the **exploit**, and Alberic repeated it; then Richard wanted to try, but the pony's patience would not endure any longer, and Alberic said he had learnt on a block of wood, and practised on the great wolf-hound. They wandered about a little longer in the court, and then climbed up the spiral stone stairs to the **battlements** at the top of the tower, where they looked at the house-tops of Rouen close beneath, and the river Seine, broadening and glittering on one side in its course to the sea, and on the other narrowing to a blue ribbon, winding through the green expanse of fertile Normandy. They threw the pebbles and bits of mortar down that they might hear them fall, and tried which could stand nearest to the edge of the battlement without **being giddy**. Richard was pleased to find that he could go the nearest, and began to tell some of Fru Astrida's stories about the **precipices** of Norway, among which when she was a young girl she used to climb about and tend the cattle in the long light summer time. When the two boys came down again into the hall to dinner, they felt as if they had known each other all their lives. The dinner was laid out in full state, and Richard had, as before, to sit in the great throne-like chair with the old Count of Harcourt on one side, but, to his comfort, Fru Astrida was on the other.

Part Two

After the dinner, Alberic de Montémar rose to take his leave, as he was to ride half way to his home that afternoon. Count Bernard, who all dinner time had been watching him intently from under his shaggy eye-brows, at this moment turned to Richard, whom he hardly ever addressed, and said to him, "Hark ye, my Lord, what should you say to have him yonder for a comrade?"

"To stay with me?" cried Richard, eagerly. "Oh, thanks, Sir Count; and may he stay?"

"You are Lord here."

"Oh, Alberic!" cried Richard, jumping out of his chair of state, and running up to him, "will you not stay with me, and be my brother and comrade?"

Alberic looked down hesitating.

"Oh, say that you will! I will give you horses, and hawks, and hounds, and I will love you–almost as well as Osmond. Oh, stay with me, Alberic."

"I must obey you, my Lord," said Alberic, "but–"

"Come, young Frenchman, out with it," said Bernard,– "no buts! Speak honestly, and at once, like a Norman, if you can."

This rough speech seemed to restore the little Baron's self-possession, and he looked up bright and bold at the rugged face of the old Dane, while he said, "I had rather not stay here."

"Ha! not do service to your Lord?"

"I would serve him with all my heart, but I do not want to stay here. I love the Castle of Montémar better, and my mother has no one but me."

"Brave and true, Sir Frenchman," said the old Count, laying his great hand on Alberic's head, and looking better pleased than Richard thought his grim features could have appeared. Then turning to Bertrand, Alberic's Seneschal, he said, "Bear the Count de Harcourt's greetings to the noble Dame de Montémar, and say to her that her son is of a free bold spirit, and if she would have him **bred up with my Lord Duke**, as his comrade and brother in arms, he will find a ready welcome."

"So, Alberic, you will come back, perhaps?" said Richard.

"That must be as my mother pleases," answered Alberic bluntly, and with all due civilities he and his Seneschal departed.

Narration and Discussion

Why is Duke Richard shy about making friends with Baron Alberic? How do the boys get over their awkwardness?

Do you think Alberic's mother will let him come and live with Richard?

For further exploration: It is interesting to note that the boys, though they are about as wealthy as any children of the time, have few "toys." (In later chapters, children do play with a ball.) What are some ways that they amuse themselves nonetheless? You might want to do a bit of exploring (online, in books, or in museums) about playthings of the middle ages, or about the games children played.

Chapter Four: In the Hands of the Frank (Part 2)

Introduction

When: A few weeks later

Where: The castle at Rouen

Alberic comes to live at the castle. King Louis also arrives, to "allow" Richard to pay homage to him; but his intentions may not be entirely kindly ones.

Vocabulary

animated: enthusiastic, energetic

left all the advantages of the game to Richard: let Richard win

with so little animation: with so little enthusiasm

vexed: annoyed, angry

courtliness of demeanour: refined manners

sit in council: participate in meetings to discuss the ruling of Normandy

the appeals from the Barons . . .: tedious financial and business matters

reproof: scolding

petted and made much of: spoiled, fussed over

mischance: bad luck

spare: thin

of a light complexion: (Note for adults) Some readers have noticed the many references to skin tone, hair, etc. in this book, and wondered if descriptions of Richard and Osmond as tall, blue-eyed, and healthy-looking, in contrast to others who are either smaller/darker or thin/pale, is meant as a subtle form of discrimination against those not fitting the "English" physical stereotype. However, arguments could be made against this, first and most obviously because Richard is of Norse background, not Anglo-Saxon; and, second, there are positive characters, such as Alberic, who are described as having darker complexions. If the question does come up, we might do worse than quote Laura Ingalls Wilder:

> She told Pa all about it, and she asked him, "You don't like golden hair better than brown, do you?"
>
> Pa's blue eyes shone down at her, and he said, "Well, Laura, my hair is brown."
>
> She had not thought of that. Pa's hair was brown, and his whiskers were brown, and she thought brown was a lovely color. (Little House in the Big Woods)

People, Places, Events

Hugh of Paris: also called Hugh the White and Hugh the Great

Count of Flanders: Arnulf, the murderer of Richard's father

Lothaire and **Carloman:** we will meet these boys soon

Part One

Four or five times a day did Richard ask Osmond and Fru Astrida if they thought Alberic would return, and it was a great satisfaction to him to find that every one agreed that it would be very foolish in the Dame de Montémar to refuse so good an offer; only Fru Astrida could not quite believe she would part with her son. Still no Baron de Montémar arrived, and the little Duke was beginning to think less about his hopes, when one evening, as he was returning from a ride with Sir Eric and Osmond, he saw four horsemen coming towards them, and a little boy in front.

"It is Alberic himself, I am sure of it!" he exclaimed, and so it proved; and while the Seneschal delivered his Lady's message to Sir Eric, Richard rode up and greeted the welcome guest.

"Oh, I am very glad your mother has sent you!"

"She said she was not fit to bring up a young warrior of the marches," said Alberic.

"Were you very sorry to come?"

"I dare say I shall not mind it soon; and Bertrand is to come and fetch me home to visit her every three months, if you will let me go, my Lord."

Richard was extremely delighted, and thought he could never do enough to make Rouen pleasant to Alberic, who after the first day or two cheered up, missed his mother less, managed to talk something between French and Norman to Sir Eric and Fru Astrida, and became a very **animated** companion and friend. In one respect Alberic was a better playfellow for the Duke than Osmond de Centeville, for Osmond, playing as a grown up man, not for his own amusement, but the child's, had **left all the advantages of the game to Richard**, who was growing not a little inclined to domineer. This Alberic did not like, unless, as he said, "it was to be always Lord and vassal, and then he did not care for the game," and he played **with so little animation** that Richard grew **vexed**.

"I can't help it," said Alberic; "if you take all the best chances to yourself, 'tis no sport for me. I will do your bidding, as you are the Duke, but I cannot like it."

"Never mind my being Duke, but play as we used to do."

"Then let us play as I did with Bertrand's sons at Montémar. I was their Baron, as you are my Duke, but my mother said there would be no sport unless we forgot all that at play."

"Then so we will. Come, begin again, Alberic, and you shall have the first turn."

However, Alberic was quite as courteous and respectful to the Duke when they were not at play, as the difference of their rank required; indeed, he had learnt much more of grace and **courtliness of demeanour** from his mother, a Provençal lady, than was yet to be found among the Normans. The Chaplain of Montémar had begun to teach him to read and write, and he liked learning much better than Richard, who would not have gone on with Father Lucas's lessons at all, if Abbot Martin of Jumièges had not put him in mind that it had been his father's especial desire.

What Richard most disliked was, however, the being obliged to **sit in council**. The Count of Harcourt did in truth govern the dukedom, but nothing could be done without the Duke's consent, and once a week at least, there was held in the great hall of Rollo's tower, what was called a *Parlement*, or "a talkation," where Count Bernard, the Archbishop, the Baron de Centeville, the Abbot of Jumièges, and such other Bishops, Nobles, or Abbots, as might chance to be at Rouen, consulted on the affairs of Normandy; and there the little Duke always was forced to be present, sitting up in his chair of state, and hearing rather than listening to, questions about the repairing and guarding of Castles, the asking of loans from the vassals, the **appeals from the Barons of the Exchequer**, who were then Nobles sent through the duchy to administer justice, and the discussions about the proceedings of his neighbours, King Louis of France, Count Foulques of Anjou, and Count Herluin of Montreuil, and how far the friendship of **Hugh of Paris**, and Alan of Brittany might be trusted.

Very tired of all this did Richard grow, especially when he found that the Normans had made up their minds not to attempt a war against the wicked **Count of Flanders**. He sighed most wearily, yawned again and again, and moved restlessly about in his chair; but whenever Count Bernard saw him doing so, he received so severe a look and sign that he grew perfectly to dread the eye of the fierce old Dane. Bernard never spoke to him to praise him, or to enter into any of his pursuits; he only treated him with the grave distant respect due to him as a Prince, or else now and then spoke a few stern words to him of **reproof** for this restlessness, or for some other childish folly.

Used as Richard was to be **petted and made much of** by the whole house of Centeville, he resented this considerably in secret, disliked and feared the old Count, and more than once told Alberic de Montémar, that as soon as he was fourteen, when he would be declared of age, he should send Count Bernard to take care of his own Castle of Harcourt, instead of letting him sit gloomy and grim in the Castle hall in the evening, spoiling all their sport.

Part Two

Winter had set in, and Osmond used daily to take the little Duke and Alberic to the nearest sheet of ice, for the Normans still prided themselves on excelling in skating, though they had long since left the frost-bound streams and lakes of Norway.

One day, as they were returning from the ice, they were surprised, even before they entered the Castle court, by hearing the trampling of horses' feet, and a sound of voices.

"What may this mean?" said Osmond. "There must surely be a great arrival of the vassals. The Duke of Brittany, perhaps."

"Oh," said Richard, piteously, "we have had one council already this week. I hope another is not coming!"

"It must import something extraordinary," proceeded Osmond. "It is a **mischance** that the Count of Harcourt is not at Rouen just now."

Richard thought this no mischance at all, and just then, Alberic, who had run on a little before, came back exclaiming, "They are French. It is the Frank tongue, not the Norman, that they speak."

"So please you, my Lord," said Osmond, stopping short, "we go not rashly into the midst of them. I would I knew what were best to do."

Osmond rubbed his forehead and stood considering, while the two boys looked at him anxiously. In a few seconds, before he had come to any conclusion, there came forth from the gate a Norman Squire, accompanied by two strangers.

"My Lord Duke," said he to Richard, in French, "Sir Eric has sent me to bring you tidings that the King of France has arrived to receive your homage."

"The King!" exclaimed Osmond.

"Ay!" proceeded the Norman, in his own tongue, "Louis himself, and with a train looking bent on mischief. I wish it may portend good to my Lord here. You see I am accompanied. I believe from my heart that Louis meant to prevent you from receiving a warning, and taking the boy out of his clutches."

"Ha! what?" said Richard, anxiously. "Why is the King come? What must I do?"

"Go on now, since there is no help for it," said Osmond. "Greet the king as becomes you, bend the knee, and pay him homage."

Richard repeated over to himself the form of homage that he might be perfect in it, and walked on into the court; Alberic, Osmond, and the rest falling back as he entered. The court was crowded with horses and men, and it was only by calling out loudly, "The Duke, the Duke," that Osmond could get space enough made for them to pass. In a few moments Richard had mounted the steps and stood in the great hall.

In the chair of state, at the upper end of the room, sat a small **spare** man, of about eight or nine-and-twenty, pale, and **of a light complexion**, with a rich dress of blue and gold. Sir Eric and several other persons stood respectfully round him, and he was conversing with the Archbishop, who, as well as Sir Eric, cast several anxious glances at the little Duke as he advanced up the hall. He came up to the King, put his knee to the ground, and was just beginning, "Louis, King of France, I–" when he found himself suddenly lifted from the ground in the King's arms, and kissed on both cheeks. Then setting him on his knee, the King exclaimed, "And is this the son of my brave and noble friend, Duke William? Ah! I should have known it from his likeness. Let me embrace you again, dear child, for your father's sake."

Richard was rather overwhelmed, but he thought the King very kind, especially when Louis began to admire his height and free-spirited bearing, and to lament that his own sons, **Lothaire** and **Carloman**, were so much smaller and more backward. He caressed Richard again and again, praised every word he said [*omission*]; and Richard began to say to himself how strange and unkind it was of Bernard de Harcourt to like to find fault with him, when, on the contrary, he deserved all this praise from the King himself.

Narration and Discussion

Does Alberic seem like a good friend for Richard? In what ways?

Why does Richard not like Count Bernard very much?

What impression do you have so far of King Louis? (Remember Duke Alan's warning about him in Chapter Three.)

Creative narration: Imagine that Alberic has access to a telephone and can call his mother. What might he say about his life in Rouen?

Chapter Five: The Faith of a King (Part 1)

Introduction

When: That night, and the next day

Where: Rouen

The Normans discover that King Louis plans to take Richard with him by force, thereby taking control of Normandy as well.

In Other News

Those reading *Trial and Triumph* will be learning about St. Anselm, who was born almost exactly a hundred years after Richard, and served as the abbot of Bec Abbey in Normandy. (Bec Abbey is located between the cities of Rouen and Bernay.)

"Knights and Days of Chivalry," in Hillyer's *A Child's History of the World*, is on the schedule for this week. The chapter introduces the topic of hunting with falcons, which will come up soon in this story..

Vocabulary

peril: danger

wiling: tricking, deceiving

all the race of Rollo: all the Normans

forsooth: a word which can mean "truly" or "can you believe it?"

our resistance will little avail: it will do us little good to resist

bear the tidings: take the message

buttress: a support of stone or brick, built against a wall

postern: back gate

burghers: townspeople

morning mass: church service

lances: spears

You will hardly break your fast: You won't get any breakfast

bring warrant: bring written permission

imperious: lordly, arrogant

gauntlet: glove

strive: struggle

turret: small tower

telling her beads: using a rosary to pray (counting off beads strung together)

insolent: rude, disrespectful

succour: help

flown into a passion: flown into temper

hold parley with them: talk to them

in ecstasy: joyfully

the Rouennais without: the townspeople outside the gates

a pledge, a hostage: someone from the French side, 'traded" for Richard, to ensure that Richard will not be harmed

***Dieu aide*:** "God helps" (a war cry)

aught of evil: anything bad

besieged: trapped

People, Places, Events

Laon: a city in Northern France. This is a hard word to pronounce for English speakers. It should be pronounced as one syllable, but with a nasal sound, as if you were going to say "long" but stopped just before the "g."

"But I thought the kings of France lived in Paris?" They did—mostly. But because of the struggles for power that were going on in France at that time, the king had moved himself and his court to **Laon** to get away from his enemies. (Louis also owned castles in the cities of Rheims and Soissons.)

"Can we visit that castle, or find photographs?" No, it has disappeared. However, there is still a large gateway called the **Porte d'Ardon**, which used to lead to the royal palace.

Reading

Part One

Duke Richard of Normandy slept in the room which had been his father's; Alberic de Montémar, as his page, slept at his feet, and Osmond de Centeville had a bed on the floor, across the door, where he lay with his sword close at hand, as his young Lord's guard and protector.

All had been asleep for some little time, when Osmond was startled by a slight movement of the door, which could not be pushed open without awakening him. In an instant he had grasped his sword, while he pressed his shoulder to the door to keep it closed; but it was his father's voice that answered him with a few whispered words in the Norse tongue, "It is I, open." He made way instantly, and old Sir Eric entered, treading cautiously with bare feet, and sat down on the bed motioning him to do the same, so that they might be able to speak lower. "Right, Osmond," he said. "It is well to be on the alert, for **peril** enough is around him–The Frank means mischief! I know from a sure hand that Arnulf of Flanders was in council with him just before he came hither, with his false tongue, **wiling** and coaxing the poor child!"

"Ungrateful traitor!" murmured Osmond. "Do you guess his purpose?"

"Yes, surely, to carry the boy off with him, and so he trusts doubtless to cut off **all the race of Rollo**! I know his purpose is to bear off the Duke, as a ward of the Crown **forsooth**. Did you not hear him luring the child with his promises of friendship with the Princes? I could not understand all his French words, but I saw it plain enough."

"You will never allow it?"

"If he does, it must be across our dead bodies; but taken as we are by surprise, **our resistance will little avail**. The Castle is full of French, the hall and court swarm with them. Even if we could draw our Normans together, we should not be more than a dozen men, and what could we do but die? That we are ready for, if it may not be otherwise, rather than let our charge be thus borne off without a pledge for his safety, and without the knowledge of the states."

"The king could not have come at a worse time," said Osmond.

"No, just when Bernard the Dane is absent. If he only knew what has befallen, he could raise the country, and come to the rescue."

"Could we not send some one to **bear the tidings** to-night?"

"I know not," said Sir Eric, musingly. "The French have taken the keeping of the doors; indeed they are so thick through the Castle that I can hardly reach one of our men, nor could I spare one hand that may avail to guard the boy tomorrow."

"Sir Eric;" a bare little foot was heard on the floor, and Alberic de Montémar stood before him. "I did not mean to listen, but I could not help hearing you. I cannot fight for the Duke yet, but I could carry a message."

"How would that be?" said Osmond, eagerly. "Once out of the Castle, and in Rouen, he could easily find means of sending [word] to the Count. He might go either to the Convent of St. Ouen, or, which would be better, to the trusty armourer, Thibault, who would soon find man and horse to send after the Count."

"Ha! let me see," said Sir Eric. "It might be. But how is he to get out?"

"I know a way," said Alberic. "I scrambled down that wide **buttress** by the east wall last week, when our ball was caught in a branch of the ivy, and the drawbridge is down."

"If Bernard knew, it would be off my mind, at least!" said Sir Eric. "Well, my young Frenchman, you may do good service."

"Osmond," whispered Alberic, as he began hastily to dress himself, "only ask one thing of Sir Eric–never to call me young Frenchman again!"

Sir Eric smiled, saying, "Prove yourself Norman, my boy."

"Then," added Osmond, "if it were possible to get the Duke himself out of the castle tomorrow morning. If I could take him forth by the **postern**, and once bring him into the town, he would be safe. It would be only to raise the **burghers**, or else to take refuge in the Church of Our Lady till the Count came up, and then Louis would find his prey out of his hands when he awoke and sought him."

"That might be," replied Sir Eric; "but I doubt your success. The French are too eager to hold him fast, to let him slip out of their hands. You will find every door guarded."

"Yes, but all the French have not seen the Duke, and the sight of a squire and a little page going forth, will scarcely excite their suspicion."

"Aye, if the Duke would bear himself like a little page; but that you need not hope for. Besides, he is so taken with this King's flatteries, that I doubt whether he would consent to leave him for the sake of Count Bernard. Poor child, he is like to be soon taught to know his true friends."

"I am ready," said Alberic, coming forward.

The Baron de Centeville repeated his instructions, and then undertook to guard the door, while his son saw Alberic set off on his expedition. Osmond went with him softly down the stairs, then avoiding the hall, which was filled with French, they crept silently to a narrow window, guarded by iron bars, placed at such short intervals apart that only so small and slim a form as Alberic's could have squeezed out between them. The distance to the ground was not much more than twice his own height, and the wall was so covered with ivy, that it was not a very dangerous feat for an active boy, so that Alberic was soon safe on the ground, then looking up to wave his cap, he ran on along the side of the moat, and was soon lost to Osmond's sight in the darkness.

Part Two

Osmond returned to the Duke's chamber, and relieved his father's guard, while Richard slept soundly on, little guessing at the plots of his enemies, or at the schemes of his faithful subjects for his protection.

Osmond thought this all the better, for he had small trust in Richard's patience and self-command, and thought there was much more chance of getting him unnoticed out of the Castle, if he did not know how much depended on it, and how dangerous his situation was.

When Richard awoke, he was much surprised at missing Alberic, but Osmond said he was gone into the town to Thibault the armourer, and this was a message on which he was so likely to be employed that Richard's suspicion was not excited. All the time he was dressing he talked about the King, and everything he meant to show him that day; then, when he was ready, the first thing was as usual to go to attend **morning mass**.

"Not by that way, to-day, my Lord," said Osmond, as Richard was about to enter the great hall. "It is crowded with the French who have been sleeping there all night; come to the postern."

Osmond turned, as he spoke, along the passage, walking fast, and not sorry that Richard was lingering a little, as it was safer for him to be first. The postern was, as he expected, guarded by two tall steel-cased figures, who immediately held their **lances** across the doorway, saying, "None passes without warrant."

"You will surely let us of the Castle attend to our daily business," said Osmond. "**You will hardly break your fast** this morning if you stop all communication with the town."

"You must **bring warrant**," repeated one of the men-at-arms. Osmond was beginning to say that he was the son of the Seneschal of the Castle, when Richard came hastily up. "What? Do these men want to stop us?" he exclaimed in the **imperious** manner he had begun to take up since his accession. "Let us go on, sirs."

The men-at-arms looked at each other, and guarded the door more closely. Osmond saw it was hopeless, and only wanted to draw his young charge back without being recognised, but Richard exclaimed loudly, "What means this?"

"The King has given orders that none should pass without warrant," was Osmond's answer. "We must wait."

"I will pass!" said Richard, impatient at opposition, to which he was little accustomed. "What mean you, Osmond? This is my Castle, and no one has a right to stop me. Do you hear, grooms? let me go. I am the Duke!"

The sentinels bowed, but all they said was, "Our orders are express."

"I tell you I am Duke of Normandy, and I will go where I please in my own city!" exclaimed Richard, passionately pressing against the crossed staves of the weapons, to force his way between them, but he was caught and held fast in the powerful **gauntlet** of one of the men-at-arms. "Let me go, villain!" cried he, struggling with all his might. "Osmond, Osmond, help!"

Even as he spoke Osmond had disengaged him from the grasp of the Frenchman, and putting his hand on his arm, said, "Nay, my Lord, it is not for you to **strive** with such as these."

"I will strive!" cried the boy. "I will not have my way barred in my own Castle. I will tell the King how these rogues of his use me. I will have them in the dungeon. Sir Eric! where is Sir Eric?"

Away he rushed to the stairs, Osmond hurrying after him, lest he should throw himself into some fresh danger, or by his loud calls attract the French, who might then easily make him prisoner. However, on the very first step of the stairs stood Sir Eric, who was too anxious for the success of the attempt to escape, to be very far off. Richard, too angry to heed where he was going, dashed up against him without seeing him, and as the old Baron took hold of him, began, "Sir Eric, Sir Eric, those French are villains! they will not let me pass–"

"Hush, hush! my Lord," said Sir Eric. "Silence! come here."

Part Three

However imperious with others, Richard from force of habit always obeyed Sir Eric, and now allowed himself to be dragged hastily and silently by him, Osmond following closely, up the stairs, up a second and a third winding flight, still narrower, and with broken steps, to a small round, thick-walled **turret** chamber, with an extremely small door, and loop-holes of windows high up in the tower. Here, to his great surprise, he found Dame Astrida, kneeling and **telling her beads**, two or three of her maidens, and about four of the Norman Squires and men-at-arms.

"So you have failed, Osmond?" said the Baron.

"But what is all this? How did Fru Astrida come up here? May I not go to the King and have those **insolent** Franks punished?"

"Listen to me, Lord Richard," said Sir Eric, "that smooth-spoken King whose words so charmed you last night is an ungrateful deceiver. The Franks have always hated and feared the Normans, and not being able to conquer us fairly, they now take to foul means. Louis came hither from Flanders; he has brought this great troop of French to surprise us, claim you as a ward of the crown, and carry you away with him to some prison of his own."

"You will not let me go?" said Richard.

"Not while I live," said Sir Eric. "Alberic is gone to warn the Count of Harcourt, to call the Normans together, and here we are ready to defend this chamber to our last breath, but we are few, the French are many, and **succour** may be far off."

"Then you meant to have taken me out of their reach this morning, Osmond?"

"Yes, my Lord."

"And if I had not **flown into a passion** and told who I was, I might have been safe! O Sir Eric! Sir Eric! you will not let me be carried off to a French prison!"

"Here, my child," said Dame Astrida, holding out her arms, "Sir Eric will do all he can for you, but we are in God's hands!"

Richard came and leant against her. "I wish I had not been in a passion!" said he, sadly, after a silence; then looking at her in wonder– "But how came you up all this way?"

"It is a long way for my old limbs," said Fru Astrida, smiling, "but my son helped me, and he deems it the only safe place in the Castle."

"The safest," said Sir Eric, "and that is not saying much for it."

Part Four

"Hark!" said Osmond, "what a tramping the Franks are making. They are beginning to wonder where the Duke is."

"To the stairs, Osmond," said Sir Eric. "On that narrow step one man may keep them at bay a long time. You can speak their [language] too, and **hold parley with them**."

"Perhaps they will think I am gone," whispered Richard, "if they cannot find me, and go away."

Osmond and two of the Normans were, as he spoke, taking their stand on the narrow spiral stair, where there was just room for one man on the step. Osmond was the lowest, the other two above him, and it would have been very hard for an enemy to force his way past them.

Osmond could plainly hear the sounds of the steps and voices of the French as they consulted together, and sought for the Duke. A man at length was heard clanking up these very stairs, till winding round, he suddenly found himself close upon young de Centeville.

"Ha! Norman!" he cried, starting back in amazement, "what are you doing here?"

"My duty," answered Osmond, shortly. "I am here to guard this stair;" and his drawn sword expressed the same intention.

The Frenchman drew back, and presently a whispering below was heard, and soon after a voice came up the stairs, saying, "Norman– good Norman–"

"What would you say?" replied Osmond, and the head of another Frank appeared. "What means all this, my friend?" was the address. "Our King comes as a guest to you, and you received him last evening as loyal vassals. Wherefore have you now drawn out of the way, and striven to bear off your young Duke into secret places? Truly it looks not well that you should thus strive to keep him apart, and therefore the King requires to see him instantly."

"Sir Frenchman," replied Osmond, "your King claims the Duke as his ward. How that may be my father knows not, but as he was committed to his charge by the states of Normandy, he holds himself bound to keep him in his own hands until further orders from them."

"That means, insolent Norman, that you intend to shut the boy up and keep him in your own rebel hands. You had best yield–it will be the better for you and for him. The child is the King's ward, and he shall not be left to be nurtured in rebellion by northern pirates."

At this moment a cry from without arose, so loud as almost to drown the voices of the speakers on the turret stair, a cry welcome to the ears of Osmond, repeated by a multitude of voices, "Haro! Haro! our little Duke!"

It was well known as a Norman shout. So just and so ready to redress all grievances had the old Duke Rollo been, that his very name was an appeal against injustice, and whenever wrong was done, the Norman outcry against the injury was always "Ha Rollo!" or as it had become shortened, "Haro." And now Osmond knew that those whose affection had been won by the uprightness of Rollo, were gathering to protect his helpless grandchild.

The cry was likewise heard by the little garrison in the turret chamber, bringing hope and joy. Richard thought himself already rescued, and springing from Fru Astrida, danced about **in ecstasy**, only longing to see the faithful Normans, whose voices he heard ringing out again and again, in calls for their little Duke, and outcries against the Franks. The windows were, however, so high, that nothing could be seen from them but the sky; and, like Richard, the old Baron de Centeville was almost beside himself with anxiety to know what force was gathered together, and what measures were being taken. He opened the door, called to his son, and asked if he could tell what was passing, but Osmond knew as little–he could see nothing but the black, cobwebbed, dusty steps winding above his head, while the clamours outside, waxing fiercer and louder, drowned all the sounds which might otherwise have come up to him from the French within the Castle.

Part Five

At last, however, Osmond called out to his father, in Norse, "There is a Frank Baron come to entreat, and this time very humbly, that the Duke may come to the King."

"Tell him," replied Sir Eric, "that save with consent of the council of Normandy, the child leaves not my hands."

"He says," called back Osmond, after a moment, "that you shall guard him yourself, with as many as you choose to bring with you. He declares on the faith of a free Baron, that the King has no thought of ill–he wants to show him to **the Rouennais without**, who are calling for him, and threaten to tear down the tower rather than not see their little Duke. Shall I bid him send a hostage?"

"Answer him," returned the Baron, "that the Duke leaves not this chamber unless a **pledge** is put into our hands for his safety. There was an oily-tongued Count, who sat next the King at supper–let him come hither, and then perchance I may trust the Duke among them."

Osmond gave the desired reply, which was carried to the King. Meantime the uproar outside grew louder than ever, and there were new sounds, a horn was winded, and there was a shout of "***Dieu aide***!" the Norman war-cry, joined with "*Notre Dame de Harcourt*!"

"There, there!" cried Sir Eric, with a long breath, as if relieved of half his anxieties, "the boy has sped well. Bernard is here at last! Now his head and hand are there, I doubt no longer."

"Here comes the Count," said Osmond, opening the door, and admitting a stout, burly man, who seemed sorely out of breath with the ascent of the steep, broken stair, and very little pleased to find himself in such a situation. The Baron de Centeville augured well from the speed with which he had been sent, thinking it proved great perplexity and distress on the part of Louis. Without waiting to hear his **hostage** speak, he pointed to a chest on which he had been sitting, and bade two of his men-at-arms stand on each side of the Count, saying at the same time to Fru Astrida, "Now, mother, if **aught of evil** befalls the child, you know your part. Come, Lord Richard."

Richard moved forward. Sir Eric held his hand. Osmond kept close behind him, and with as many of the men-at-arms as could be spared from guarding Fru Astrida and her hostage, he descended the stairs, not by any means sorry to go, for he was weary of being **besieged** in that turret chamber, whence he could see nothing, and with those friendly cries in his ears, he could not be afraid.

Narration and Discussion

Why did the plan to get Richard out of the castle fail?

What might happen if the Normans refuse to let Richard go downstairs to see the King?

For further thought: We are told that Osmond had "small trust in Richard's patience and self-command." What does he mean by "self-command?" What small step does Richard make towards gaining more of this?

Creative narration: Imagine that you are a news reporter who can go anywhere in or around the castle. Who might you speak to, and what would they say? (Examples: Fru Astrida in the tower; one of the townspeople outside; or the French count who has to sit in the tower until Richard returns safely.)

Chapter Five: The Faith of a King (Part 2)

Introduction

When: The same day

Where: Rouen

The Normans insist that King Louis swear to be Richard's friend and protector, which he then takes as permission to take Richard home to his own castle. Bernard the Dane promises the King that "as thou keepest that oath to the fatherless child, so may the Lord do unto thine house!" (Perhaps it's a promise, perhaps it's a warning.)

Vocabulary

paler than his wont: even paler than he usually looked

lull in the tumult: pause in the noise

rascaille: "riff-raff"; rough people

incensed: angry

appease them: make them happy

on the faith of a King: This is also the title of the chapter. What do you think it means?

burgesses: townspeople, citizens

wistfully: longingly

onset: attack

rue the day: be very sorry for

long keels: war ships

chivalry: the system of knighthood, with all its skills and manners

happy: fortunate, blessed

wrested: taken forcefully

tarry: stay

ready of counsel: clear-minded, quick-witted

exhorted: urged

the bar-tailed falcon: The boys seem to have been training a falcon (hunting bird) together.

People, Places, Events

King Harald Bluetooth: The king of Denmark and Norway; there will be a longer explanation about him later on

Hugh the White, Count of Paris: Duke of the Franks and Count of Paris, which made him a very powerful man. He was the brother-in-law of King Louis; however, they were often in conflict.

Hubert of Senlis [sahn-leese]: A French nobleman, probably the great-uncle of Richard

Queen Gerberge (zhair-bairzh): or Gerberga; the wife of Louis

Reading

Part One

He was conducted to the large council-room which was above the hall. There, the King was walking up and down anxiously, looking **paler than his wont**, and no wonder, for the uproar sounded tremendous there–and now and then a stone dashed against the sides of the deep window.

Nearly at the same moment as Richard entered by one door, Count Bernard de Harcourt came in from the other, and there was a slight **lull in the tumult**.

"What means this, my Lords?" exclaimed the King. "Here am I come in all good will, in memory of my warm friendship with Duke William, to take on me the care of his orphan, and hold council with you for avenging his death, and is this the greeting you afford me? You steal away the child, and stir up the **rascaille** of Rouen against me. Is this the reception for your King?"

"Sir King," replied Bernard, "what your intentions may be, I know not. All I do know is, that the burghers of Rouen are fiercely **incensed** against you–so much so, that they were almost ready to tear me to pieces for being absent at this juncture. They say that you are keeping the child prisoner in his own Castle and that they will have him restored if they tear it down to the foundations."

"You are a true man, a loyal man–you understand my good intentions," said Louis, trembling, for the Normans were extremely dreaded. "You would not bring the shame of rebellion on your town and people. Advise me–I will do just as you counsel me–how shall I **appease them**?"

"Take the child, lead him to the window, swear that you mean him no evil, that you will not take him from us," said Bernard. "Swear it **on the faith of a King**."

"As a King–as a Christian, it is true!" said Louis. "Here, my boy! Wherefore shrink from me? What have I done, that you should fear me? You have been listening to evil tales of me, my child. Come hither."

At a sign from the Count de Harcourt, Sir Eric led Richard forward, and put his hand into the King's. Louis took him to the window, lifted him upon the sill, and stood there with his arm round him, upon which the shout, "Long live Richard, our little Duke!" arose again. Meantime, the two Centevilles looked in wonder at the old Harcourt, who shook his head and muttered in his own tongue, "I will do all I may, but our force is small, and the King has the best of it. We must not yet bring a war on ourselves."

"Hark! he is going to speak," said Osmond.

"Fair Sirs!–excellent **burgesses**!" began the King, as the cries lulled a little. "I rejoice to see the love ye bear to our young Prince! I would all my subjects were equally loyal! But wherefore dread me, as if I were come to injure him? I, who came but to take counsel how to avenge the death of his father, who brought me back from England when I was a friendless exile. Know ye not how deep is the debt of gratitude I owe to Duke William? He it was who made me King–it was he who gained me the love of the King of Germany; he stood godfather for my son–to him I owe all my wealth and state, and all my care is to [repay it] to his child, since, alas! I may not to himself. Duke William rests in his bloody grave! It is for me to call his murderers to account, and to cherish his son, even as mine own!"

So saying, Louis tenderly embraced the little boy, and the Rouennais below broke out into another cry, in which "Long live King Louis," was joined with "Long live Richard!"

"You will not let the child go?" said Eric, meanwhile, to Harcourt.

"Not without provision for his safety, but we are not fit for war as yet, and to let him go is the only means of warding it off."

Eric groaned and shook his head; but the Count de Harcourt's judgment was of such weight with him, that he never dreamt of disputing it.

"Bring me here," said the King, "all that you deem most holy, and you shall see me pledge myself to be your Duke's most faithful friend."

There was some delay, during which the Norman Nobles had time for further counsel together, and Richard looked **wistfully** at them, wondering what was to happen to him, and wishing he could venture to ask for Alberic.

Several of the Clergy of the Cathedral presently appeared in procession, bringing with them the book of the Gospels on which

Richard had taken his installation oath, with others of the sacred treasures of the Church, preserved in gold cases. The Priests were followed by a few of the Norman Knights and Nobles, some of the burgesses of Rouen, and, to Richard's great joy, by Alberic de Montémar himself. The two boys stood looking eagerly at each other, while preparation was made for the ceremony of the King's oath.

Part Two

The stone table in the middle of the room was cleared, and arranged so as in some degree to resemble the Altar in the Cathedral; then the Count de Harcourt, standing before it, and holding the King's hand, demanded of him whether he would undertake to be the friend, protector, and good Lord of Richard, Duke of Normandy, guarding him from all his enemies, and ever seeking his welfare. Louis, with his hand on the Gospels, "swore that so he would."

"Amen!" returned Bernard the Dane, solemnly, "and as thou keepest that oath to the fatherless child, so may the Lord do unto thine house!"

Then followed the ceremony, which had been interrupted the night before, of the homage and oath of allegiance which Richard owed to the King, and, on the other hand, the King's formal reception of him as a vassal, holding, under him, the two dukedoms of Normandy and Brittany. "And," said the King, raising him in his arms and kissing him, "no dearer vassal do I hold in all my realm than this fair child, son of my murdered friend and benefactor–precious to me as my own children, as so on my Queen and I hope to testify."

Richard did not much like all this embracing; but he was sure the King really meant him no ill, and he wondered at all the distrust the Centevilles had shown.

"Now, brave Normans," said the King, "be ye ready speedily, for an **onset** on the traitor Fleming. The cause of my ward is my own cause. Soon shall the trumpet be sounded, the [men be called to battle], and Arnulf, in the flames of his cities, and the blood of his vassals, shall learn to **rue the day** when his foot trod the Isle of Pecquigny! How many Normans can you bring to the muster, Sir Count?"

"I cannot say, within a few hundreds of lances," replied the old Dane, cautiously; "it depends on the numbers that may be engaged in the Italian war with the Saracens, but of this be sure, Sir King, that every man in Normandy and Brittany who can draw a sword or bend a bow, will stand forth in the cause of our little Duke; aye, and that his blessed father's memory is held so dear in our northern home, that it needs but a message to **King Harald Bluetooth** to bring a fleet of **long keels** into the Seine, with stout Danes enough to carry fire and sword, not merely through Flanders, but through all France. We of the North are not apt to forget old friendships and favours, Sir King."

"Yes, yes, I know the Norman faith of old," returned Louis, uneasily, "but we should scarcely need such wild allies as you propose; the **Count of Paris**, and Hubert of Senlis may be reckoned on, I suppose."

"No truer friend to Normandy than gallant and wise old **Hugh the White**!" said Bernard, "and as to Senlis, he is uncle to the boy, and doubly bound to us."

"I rejoice to see your confidence," said Louis. "You shall soon hear from me. In the meantime I must return to gather my force together, and summon my great vassals, and I will, with your leave, brave Normans, take with me my dear young ward. His presence will plead better in his cause than the finest words; moreover, he will grow up in love and friendship with my two boys, and shall be nurtured with them in all good learning and **chivalry**, nor shall he ever be reminded that he is an orphan while under the care of **Queen Gerberge** and myself."

"Let the child come to me, so please you, my Lord the King," answered Harcourt, bluntly. "I must hold some converse with him, ere I can reply."

"Go then, Richard," said Louis, "go to your trusty vassal–**happy** are you in possessing such a friend; I hope you know his value."

"Here then, young Sir," said the Count, in his native tongue, when Richard had crossed from the King's side, and stood beside him, "what say you to this proposal?"

"The King is very kind," said Richard. "I am sure he is kind; but I do not like to go from Rouen, or from Dame Astrida."

"Listen, my Lord," said the Dane, stooping down and speaking low. "The King is resolved to have you away; he has with him the best of his Franks, and has so taken us at unawares, that though I might yet rescue you from his hands, it would not be without a fierce struggle, wherein you might be harmed, and this castle and town certainly burnt, and **wrested** from us. A few weeks or months, and we shall have time to draw our force together, so that Normandy need fear no man, and for that time you must **tarry** with him."

"Must I–and all alone?"

"No, not alone, not without the most trusty guardian that can be found for you. Friend Eric, what say you?" and he laid his hand on the old Baron's shoulder. "Yet, I know not; true thou art, as a Norwegian mountain, but I doubt me if thy brains are not too dull to see through the French wiles and disguises, sharp as thou didst show thyself last night."

"That was Osmond, not I," said Sir Eric. "He knows [their tongue] better than I. He [would be] the best to go with the poor child, if go he must."

"Bethink you, Eric," said the Count, in an undertone, "Osmond is the only hope of your good old house–if there is foul play, the guardian will be the first to suffer."

"Since you think fit to peril the only hope of all Normandy, I am not the man to hold back my son where he may aid him," said old Eric, sadly. "The poor child will be lonely and uncared-for there, and it were hard he should not have one faithful comrade and friend with him."

"It is well," said Bernard. "Young as he is, I had rather trust Osmond with the child than any one else, for he is **ready of counsel**, and quick of hand."

"Aye, and a pretty pass it is come to," muttered old Centeville, "that we, whose business it is to guard the boy, should send him where you scarcely like to trust my son."

Bernard paid no further attention to him, but, coming forward, required another oath from the King, that Richard should be as safe and free at his court as at Rouen, and that on no pretence whatsoever should he be taken from under the immediate care of his Esquire, Osmond Fitz Eric, heir of Centeville.

Part Three

After this, the King was impatient to depart, and all was preparation. Bernard called Osmond aside to give full instructions on his conduct, and the means of communicating with Normandy; and Richard was taking leave of Fru Astrida, who had now descended from her turret, bringing her hostage with her. She wept much over her little Duke, praying that he might safely be restored to Normandy, even though she might not live to see it; she **exhorted** him not to forget the good and holy learning in which he had been brought up, to rule his temper, and, above all, to say his prayers constantly [*omission*]. As to her own grandson, anxiety for him seemed almost lost in her fears for Richard, and the chief things she said to him, when he came to take leave of her, were directions as to the care he was to take of the child, telling him the honour he now received was one which would make his name forever esteemed if he did but fulfil his trust, the most precious that Norman had ever yet received.

"I will, grandmother, to the very best of my power," said Osmond; "I may die in his cause, but never will I be faithless!"

"Alberic!" said Richard, "are you glad to be going back to Montémar?"

"Yes, my Lord," answered Alberic, sturdily, "as glad as you will be to come back to Rouen."

"Then I shall send for you directly, Alberic, for I shall never love the Princes Carloman and Lothaire half as well as you!"

"My Lord the King is waiting for the Duke," said a Frenchman, coming forward.

"Farewell then, Fru Astrida. Do not weep. I shall soon come back. Farewell, Alberic. Take **the bar-tailed falcon** back to Montémar, and keep him for my sake. Farewell, Sir Eric–Farewell, Count Bernard. When the Normans come to conquer Arnulf you will lead them. O dear, dear Fru Astrida, farewell again."

"Farewell, my own darling. The blessing of Heaven go with you, and bring you safe home! Farewell, Osmond. Heaven guard you and strengthen you to be his shield and his defence!"

Narration and Discussion

Why does Richard have to go with King Louis? How are the Normans planning to get him home again?

For further thought: Count Bernard pays Osmond a great compliment when he says, "Young as he is, I had rather trust Osmond with the child than any one else, for he is ready of counsel, and quick of hand." What does he mean?

Creative narration: When Alberic returns to Montémar, what might he tell his mother about what has happened?

Chapter Six: The Playfellow of Princes (Part 1)

Introduction

When: Shortly after the last chapter

Where: The journey, and the arrival at the castle of Laon

Richard is not impressed by the French countryside they are passing through; and his stay at the royal palace doesn't start off very well either.

A Tangled Web of Facts and Dates

While Richard's relationship with the sons of King Louis forms a major part of this book, it seems historically impossible, as Prince Lothaire (sometimes spelled Lothair) was not born until 941 A.D., making him only a toddler during these years.

"Carloman," the younger brother, is properly named Charles, the Duke of Lower Lorraine, and he is said to have been born in 953 A.D. However, it is also stated that Charles (and not Lothaire) was sent as a hostage when his father was captured by the Normans in 945, which again is impossible!

Perhaps it is best just to go on with the story.

Vocabulary

palfrey: horse

rude: simple, plain

most goodly: best, wealthiest

traverse: cross

did not find the second place left for him at the board: he should have had the second-best seat (after the King) at the dinner table

morass: swamp

Fru Astrida's story of the golden bracelets: A historian named William of Jumièges wrote a book called "Deeds of the Norman Dukes," which includes this tale about Rollo. One day he was out hunting, and hung his golden bracelets on an oak tree. The bracelets stayed on the tree for three years, showing not only the fear the Normans had of Rollo, but the safety in which they lived.

aguish: unhealthy, ill-looking

iron collars round their necks: The collars show that these people were serfs: poor farming people who were "owned" by the local lord, but who also had to pay him rent.

cornfields: fields of grain

staff: walking stick

the fleur-de-lys standard: the French flag with symbols of lilies on it

perform his obeisance: pay his respects, make his bows

affronted: offended

old Rollo and Charles the Simple: Do you remember what happened when Rollo was asked to kiss the king's foot?

imperious: arrogant, domineering

People, Places, Events

Lothaire, Carloman: the sons of King Louis and Queen Gerberge

Reading

Part One

Away from the tall narrow gateway of Rollo's Tower, with the cluster of friendly, sorrowful faces looking forth from it, away from the booth-like shops of Rouen, and the stout burghers shouting with all the power of their lungs, "Long live Duke Richard! Long live King Louis! Death to the Fleming!"–away from the broad Seine–away from home and friends, rode the young Duke of Normandy, by the side of the **palfrey** of the King of France.

The King took much notice of him, kept him by his side, talked to him, admired the beautiful cattle grazing in security in the green pastures, and, as he looked at the rich dark brown earth of the fields, the Castles towering above the woods, the Convents looking like great farms, the many villages round the **rude** Churches, and the numerous population who came out to gaze at the party, and repeat the cry of "Long live the King! Blessings on the little Duke!" he told Richard, again and again, that his was the **most goodly** duchy in France and Germany to boot.

When they crossed the Epte, the King would have Richard in the same boat with him, and sitting close to Louis, and talking eagerly about falcons and hounds, the little Duke passed the boundary of his own dukedom.

The country beyond was not like Normandy. First they came to a great forest, which seemed to have no path through it. The King ordered that one of the men, who had rowed them across, should be made to serve as guide, and two of the men-at-arms took him between them, and forced him to lead the way, while others, with their swords and battle-axes, cut down and cleared away the tangled branches and briars that nearly choked the path. All the time, every one was sharply on the look-out for robbers, and the weapons were all held ready for use at a moment's notice. On getting beyond the forest a Castle rose before them, and, though it was not yet late in the day, they resolved to rest there, as a marsh lay not far before them, which it would not have been safe to **traverse** in the evening twilight.

Part Two

The Baron of the Castle received them with great respect to the King, but without paying much attention to the Duke of Normandy, and Richard **did not find the second place left for him at the board**. He coloured violently, and looked first at the King, and then at Osmond, but Osmond held up his finger in warning; he remembered how he had lost his temper before, and what had come of it, and resolved to try to bear it better; and just then the Baron's daughter, a gentle-looking maiden of fifteen or sixteen, came and spoke to him, and entertained him so well, that he did not think much more of his offended dignity.

When they set off on their journey again, the Baron and several of his followers came with them to show the only safe way across the **morass**, and a very slippery, treacherous, quaking road it was, where the horses' feet left pools of water wherever they trod. The King and the Baron rode together, and the other French Nobles closed round them; Richard was left quite in the background, and though the French men-at-arms took care not to lose sight of him, no one offered him any assistance, excepting Osmond, who, giving his own horse to Sybald, one of the two Norman grooms who accompanied him, led Richard's horse by the bridle along the whole distance of the marshy path, a business that could scarcely have been pleasant, as Osmond wore his heavy hauberk, and his pointed, iron-guarded boots sunk deep at every step into the bog. He spoke little, but seemed to be taking good heed of every stump of willow or stepping-stone that might serve as a note of remembrance of the path.

At the other end of the morass began a long tract of dreary-looking, heathy waste, without a sign of life. The Baron took leave of the King, only sending three men-at-arms, to show him the way to a monastery, which was to be the next halting-place. He sent three, because it was not safe for one, even fully armed, to ride alone, for fear of the attacks of the followers of a certain marauding Baron, who was at deadly feud with him, and made all that border a most perilous region. Richard might well observe that he did not like [this country] half as well as Normandy, and that the people ought to learn **Fru Astrida's story of the golden bracelets**, which, in his grandfather's time, had hung untouched for a year, in a tree in a forest.

Part Three

It was pretty much the same through the whole journey, waste lands, marshes, and forests alternated. The Castles stood on high mounds frowning on the country round, and villages were clustered round them, where the people either fled away, driving off their cattle with them at the first sight of an armed band, or else, if they remained, proved to be thin, wretched-looking creatures, with wasted limbs, **aguish** faces, and often **iron collars round their necks**. Wherever there was anything of more prosperous appearance, such as a few **cornfields**, vineyards on the slopes of the hills, fat cattle, and peasantry looking healthy and secure, there was sure to be seen a range of long low stone buildings, surmounted with crosses, with a short square Church tower rising in the midst, and interspersed with gnarled hoary old apple-trees, or with gardens of pot-herbs spreading before them to the meadows. If, instead of two or three men-at-arms from a Castle, or of some trembling serf pressed into the service, and beaten, threatened, and watched to prevent treachery, the King asked for a guide at a Convent, some lay brother would take his **staff**; or else mount an ass, and proceed in perfect confidence and security as to his return homewards, sure that his poverty and his sacred character would alike protect him from any outrage from the most lawless marauder of the neighbourhood.

Thus they travelled until they reached the royal Castle of Laon, where **the Fleur-de-Lys standard** on the battlements announced the presence of Gerberge, Queen of France, and her two sons. The King rode first into the court with his Nobles, and before Richard could follow him through the narrow arched gateway, he had dismounted, entered the Castle, and was out of sight. Osmond held the Duke's stirrup, and followed him up the steps which led to the Castle Hall. It was full of people, but no one made way, and Richard, holding his Squire's hand, looked up in his face, inquiring and bewildered.

Part Four

"Sir Seneschal," said Osmond, seeing a broad portly old man, with grey hair and a golden chain, "this is the Duke of Normandy–I pray you conduct him to the King's presence."

Richard had no longer any cause to complain of neglect, for the Seneschal instantly made him a very low bow, and calling "Place–place for the high and mighty Prince, my Lord Duke of Normandy!" ushered him up to the dais or raised part of the floor, where the King and Queen stood together talking. The Queen looked round, as Richard was announced, and he saw her face, which was sallow, and with a sharp sour expression that did not please him, and he backed and looked reluctant, while Osmond, with a warning hand pressed on his shoulder, was trying to remind him that he ought to go forward, kneel on one knee, and kiss her hand.

"There he is," said the King.

"One thing secure!" said the Queen; "but what makes that northern giant keep close to his heels?"

Louis answered something in a low voice, and, in the meantime, Osmond tried in a whisper to induce his young Lord to go forward and **perform his obeisance**.

"I tell you I will not," said Richard. "She looks cross, and I do not like her." Luckily he spoke his own language; but his look and air expressed a good deal of what he said, and Gerberge looked all the more unattractive.

"A thorough little Norwegian bear," said the King; "fierce and unruly as the rest. Come, and perform your courtesy–do you forget where you are?" he added, sternly. Richard bowed, partly because Osmond forced down his shoulder; but he thought of **old Rollo and Charles the Simple**, and his proud heart resolved that he would never kiss the hand of that sour-looking Queen. It was a determination made in pride and defiance, and he suffered for it afterwards; but no more passed now, for the Queen only saw in his behaviour that of an unmannerly young Northman: and though she disliked and despised him, she did not care enough about his courtesy to insist on its being paid. She sat down, and so did the King, and they went on talking; the King probably telling her his adventures at Rouen, while Richard stood on the step of the dais, swelling with sullen pride.

Part Five

Nearly a quarter of an hour had passed in this manner when the servants came to set the table for supper, and Richard, in spite of his indignant looks, was forced to stand aside. He wondered that all this time he had not seen the two Princes, thinking how strange he should have thought it, to let his own dear father be in the house so long without coming to welcome him. At last, just as the supper had been served up, a side door opened, and the Seneschal called, "Place for the high and mighty Princes, my Lord **Lothaire** and my Lord **Carloman**!" and in walked two boys, one about the same age as Richard, the other rather less than a year younger. They were both thin, pale, sharp-featured children, and Richard drew himself up to his full height, with great satisfaction at being so much taller than Lothaire.

They came up ceremoniously to their father and kissed his hand, while he kissed their foreheads, and then said to them, "There is a new play-fellow for you."

"Is that the little Northman?" said Carloman, turning to stare at Richard with a look of curiosity, while Richard in his turn felt considerably **affronted** that a boy so much less than himself should call him little.

"Yes," said the Queen; "your father has brought him home with him." Carloman stepped forward, shyly holding out his hand to the stranger, but his brother pushed him rudely aside. "I am the eldest; it is my business to be first. So, young Northman, you are come here for us to play with."

Richard was too much amazed at being spoken to in this **imperious** way to make any answer. He was completely taken by surprise, and only opened his great blue eyes to their utmost extent.

"Ha! why don't you answer? Don't you hear? Can you speak only your own heathen tongue?" continued Lothaire.

"The Norman is no heathen tongue!" said Richard, at once breaking silence in a loud voice. "We are as good Christians as you are–ay, and better too."

"Hush! hush! my Lord!" said Osmond.

"What now, Sir Duke," again interfered the King, in an angry tone, "are you brawling already? Time, indeed, I should take you from your own savage court. Sir Squire, look to it, that you keep your charge in better rule, or I shall send him instantly to bed, supperless."

"My Lord, my Lord," whispered Osmond, "see you not that you are bringing discredit on all of us?"

"I would be courteous enough, if they would be courteous to me," returned Richard, gazing with eyes full of defiance at Lothaire, who, returning an angry look, had nevertheless shrunk back to his mother. She meanwhile was saying, "So strong, so rough, the young savage is, he will surely harm our poor boys!"

"Never fear," said Louis; "he shall be watched. And," he added in a lower tone, "for the present, at least, we must keep up appearances. Hubert of Senlis, and Hugh of Paris, have their eyes on us, and were the boy to be missed, the grim old Harcourt would have all the pirates of his land on us in the twinkling of an eye. We have him, and there we must rest content for the present. Now to supper."

Narration and Discussion

What surprised Richard most during the journey to Laon?

Why did the King call Richard a "Norwegian bear?"

Creative narration: Draw a picture of Richard's first meeting with the king's family.

For further exploration: Just for fun, you might want to look for a book of manners, and practice polite introductions. A classic (and short!) book on the subject is *Manners Can Be Fun* by Munro Leaf. Some may also enjoy the humour of *What Do You Say, Dear?* and *What Do You Do, Dear?* by Sesyle Joslin, although there are one or two examples that grownups might not entirely like, so we advise pre-reading. A more recent book (that covers new situations like pet etiquette) is Heather Hammonds' *My book of manners: a lift the flap book.*

Chapter Six: The Playfellow of Princes (Part 2)

Introduction

When: That evening

Where: The castle at Laon

Richard makes friends with one of the princes; but he still finds the French-style castle a strange place. "Glass windows and hangings to sleeping chambers! I do not like it; I am sure we shall never be able to sleep, closed up from the free air of heaven in this way…"

Vocabulary

I shall be nine: Historical records say that Richard was born in the year 932, which would make him ten rather than nine.

on the eve of St. Boniface: the feast day of St. Boniface is June 5

Martinmas: the feast of St. Martin of Tours, on November 11

scourged: whipped

fresh rushes strewn about the floor: Generally, the rushes covering medieval floors weren't changed very often, and they became very dirty and smelly. Fresh rushes must have seemed like luxury accommodations, especially for those who had to sleep on the floor.

oratory: chapel

chanting his matins: performing the morning religious ceremony

glazing: glass windows

casements: windows on hinges

tell your beads: say your prayers with a rosary

crib: bed

People, Places, Events

Sybald and **Henry:** two Norman grooms (servants caring for horses) who had travelled with Richard and Osmond

Reading

Part One

At supper, Richard sat next little Carloman, who peeped at him every now and then from under his eyelashes, as if he was afraid of him; and presently, when there was a good deal of talking going on, so that his voice could not be heard, half whispered, in a very grave tone, "Do you like salt beef or fresh?"

"I like fresh," answered Richard, with equal gravity, "only we eat salt all the winter."

There was another silence, and then Carloman, with the same solemnity, asked, "How old are you?"

"**I shall be nine on the eve of St. Boniface**. How old are you?"

"Eight. I was eight at **Martinmas**, and Lothaire was nine three days since."

Another silence; then, as Osmond waited on Richard, Carloman returned to the charge, "Is that your Squire?"

"Yes, that is Osmond de Centeville."

"How tall he is!"

"We Normans are taller than you French."

"Don't say so to Lothaire, or you will make him angry."

"Why? it is true."

"Yes; but–" and Carloman sunk his voice– "there are some things which Lothaire will not hear said. Do not make him cross, or he will make my mother displeased with you. She caused Thierry de Lincourt to be **scourged**, because his ball hit Lothaire's face."

"She cannot scourge me–I am a free Duke," said Richard. "But why? Did he do it on purpose?"

"Oh, no!"

"And was Lothaire hurt?"

"Hush! you must say Prince Lothaire. No; it was quite a soft ball."

"Why?" again asked Richard– "why was he scourged?"

"I told you, because he hit Lothaire."

"Well, but did he not laugh, and say it was nothing? Alberic quite knocked me down with a great snowball the other day, and Sir Eric laughed, and said I must stand firmer."

"Do you make snowballs?"

"To be sure I do! Do not you?"

"Oh, no! the snow is so cold."

"Ah! you are but a little boy," said Richard, in a superior manner.

Carloman asked how it was done; and Richard gave an animated description of the snowballing, a fortnight ago, at Rouen, when Osmond and some of the other young men built a snow fortress, and defended it against Richard, Alberic, and the other Squires. Carloman listened with delight, and declared that next time it snowed, they would have a snow castle; and thus, by the time supper was over, the two little boys were very good friends.

Part Two

Bedtime came not long after supper. Richard's was a smaller room than he had been used to at Rouen; but it amazed him exceedingly when he first went into it: he stood gazing in wonder, because, as he said, "It was as if he had been in a church."

"Yes, truly!" said Osmond. "No wonder these poor creatures of French cannot stand before a Norman lance, if they cannot sleep without glass to their windows. Well! what would my father say to this?"

"And see! see, Osmond! they have put hangings up all round the walls, just like Our Lady's church on a great feast-day. They treat us just as if we were the holy saints; and here are **fresh rushes strewn about the floor**, too. This must be a mistake–it must be an **oratory**, instead of my chamber."

"No, no, my Lord; here is our gear, which I bade **Sybald** and **Henry** [bring to] our chamber. Well, these Franks are come to a pass, indeed! My grandmother will never believe what we shall have to tell her. Glass windows and hangings to sleeping chambers! I do not like it I am sure we shall never be able to sleep, closed up from the free air of heaven in this way: I shall be always waking, and fancying I am in the chapel at home, hearing Father Lucas **chanting his matins**. Besides, my father would blame me for letting you be made as tender as a Frank. I'll have out this precious window, if I can."

Luxurious as the young Norman thought the King, the **glazing** of Laon was not permanent. It consisted of **casements**, which could be put up or removed at pleasure; for, as the court possessed only one set of glass windows, they were taken down, and carried from place to place, as often as Louis removed from Rheims to Soissons, Laon, or any other of his royal castles; so that Osmond did not find much difficulty in displacing them, and letting in the sharp, cold, wintry breeze.

Part Three

The next thing he did was to give his young Lord a lecture on his want of courtesy, telling him that "no wonder the Franks thought he had no more culture than a Viking (or pirate), fresh caught from Norway. A fine notion he was giving them of the training he had at Centeville, if he could not even show common civility to the Queen–a lady! Was that the way Alberic had behaved when he came to Rouen?"

"Fru Astrida did not make sour faces at him, nor call him a young savage," replied Richard.

"No, and he gave her no reason to do so; he knew that the first teaching of a young Knight is to be courteous to ladies–never mind whether fair and young, or old and foul of favour. Till you learn and note that, Lord Richard, you will never be worthy of your golden spurs."

"And the King told me she would treat me as a mother," exclaimed Richard. "Do you think the King speaks the truth, Osmond?"

"That we shall see by his deeds," said Osmond.

"He was very kind while we were in Normandy. I loved him so much better than the Count de Harcourt; but now I think that the Count is best! I'll tell you, Osmond, I will never call him grim old Bernard again."

"You had best not, sir, for you will never have a more true-hearted vassal."

"Well, I wish we were back in Normandy, with Fru Astrida and Alberic. I cannot bear that Lothaire. He is proud, and unknightly, and cruel. I am sure he is, and I will never love him."

"Hush, my Lord!–beware of speaking so loud. You are not in your own Castle."

"And Carloman is a chicken-heart," continued Richard, unheeding. "He does not like to touch snow, and he cannot even slide on the ice, and he is afraid to go near that great dog–that beautiful wolf-hound."

"He is very little," said Osmond.

"I am sure I was not as cowardly at his age, now was I, Osmond? Don't you remember?"

"Come, Lord Richard, I cannot let you wait to remember everything; **tell your beads** and pray that we may be brought safe back to Rouen; and that you may not forget all the good that Father Lucas and holy Abbot Martin have laboured to teach you."

So Richard told the beads of his rosary–black polished wood, with amber at certain spaces–he repeated a prayer with every bead, and Osmond did the same; then the little Duke put himself into a narrow **crib** of richly carved walnut; while Osmond, having stuck his dagger so as to form an additional bolt to secure the door, and examined the hangings that no secret entrance might be concealed behind them, gathered a heap of rushes together, and lay down on them, wrapped in his mantle, across the doorway. The Duke was soon asleep; but the Squire lay long awake, musing on the possible dangers that surrounded his charge, and on the best way of guarding against them.

Narration and Discussion

Richard has a new friend and a comfortable room—perhaps things won't be too bad after all at Laon. What do you think?

Osmond reminds Richard that "the first teaching of a young knight is to be courteous to ladies." What other rules of courtesy do you think are important for today's "young knights" (and young ladies)? (See the previous lesson for some books about manners.)

For further thought: Richard seems to be having second thoughts about King Louis and Bernard de Harcourt. Why do you think he has changed his mind?

For further exploration (do you want to build a snowman?): While the story about playing with snowballs "the other day" is amusing, it is unlikely. As Richard travelled to Laon, he saw "beautiful cattle grazing in security in the green pastures, and… the rich dark brown earth of the fields," so it doesn't sound like it was winter in France. Even in

Normandy, at least in our day, there can be some snow (in the coldest part of winter), but it doesn't usually last long. Another clue that perhaps our author wasn't thinking about the seasons very carefully is that Richard remembers being at Rouen last Christmas with his father; but Christmas hasn't yet come around again. **However:** when it did snow during the Middle Ages, both adults and children liked to make snowballs, go sledding, and even skate on pieces of polished wood or bone. The website of "Professor Sarah Peverley," for example, contains a number of images of "Medieval Winter Sports."

Creative narration: As you are now at the end of the first term and may be preparing for examinations, this would be a good time to tell, or draw, or make a model of some part of the story so far. What was your favourite scene? What do you remember best?

Examination Questions for *The Little Duke*, Term 1

Choose one or more of these questions to answer.

1. How did Richard get to be the Duke of Normandy, although he was just a boy?

2. Why did the escape attempt at Rouen fail? Tell the whole story.

3. Tell how Richard was taken to live at the royal palace.

Chapter Seven: Captors and Captive (Part 1)

Introduction

When: The same year

Where: The royal castle at Laon

In this chapter, we learn about Prince Lothaire's bullying ways and his cruelty to animals. (Warning for those with younger ones: he becomes angry at his dog and orders it killed, and then attempts to have a falcon's eyes put out). When Richard interferes in one such incident, he ends up being injured himself.

In Other News

If you are reading *Trial and Triumph*, this week you will read about St. Bernard of Clairvaux (1090-1153 A.D.), the founder of a monastery in northeastern France. Among other things, he was the author of hymns which are still sung today, such as "Jesus, The Very Thought of Thee."

Let's Talk About Falcons

If you are reading Hillyer's *A Child's History of the* World, the chapter "Knights and Days of Chivalry" would be useful here, as it mentions the use of falcons. There are many other books and videos that describe falconry, but a warning about this for very sensitive children: falcons are trained to hunt small animals such as squirrels, rabbits, and smaller birds, so videos about hunting might not be for the squeamish. A novel to read for students who are interested in falconry is *My Side of the Mountain* by Jean Craighead George (suggested as a reading practice option in AO Years Three and Four).

Vocabulary

"as became his rank": as was proper for his rank of Duke

puny: weak, small

kindred by blood: family, relatives

check his faults: stop him from behaving like that

falcon: see note above

abated: lessened

consternation: noise, confusion

leisure to feel the smarting: time to feel the pain

Berserkers: Scandinavian warriors in ancient times who were known for fighting in a frenzy of rage and fury. The word **Berserker** literally means "bear shirt."

effeminate: having feminine manners

slander: telling lies about someone

meanest: lowest

the poor boys: the "unfortunate children who were [Lothaire's] playfellows"

People, Places, Events

Sieur de Centeville: the French way to say Lord Centeville (referring to Osmond)

Reading

Part One

Osmond de Centeville was soon convinced that no immediate peril threatened his young Duke at the Court of Laon. Louis seemed to intend to fulfil his oaths to the Normans by allowing the child to be the companion of his own sons, and to be treated in every respect **as became his rank**. Richard had his proper place at table, and all due attendance; he learnt, rode, and played with the Princes, and there was nothing to complain of, excepting the coldness and inattention with which the King and Queen treated him, by no means fulfilling the promise of being "as parents" to their orphan ward. Gerberge, who had from the first dreaded his superior strength and his roughness with her **puny** boys, and who had been by no means won by his manners at their first meeting, was especially distant and severe with him, hardly ever speaking to him except with some rebuke, which, it must be confessed, Richard often deserved.

As to the boys, his constant companions, Richard was on very friendly terms with Carloman, a gentle, timid, weakly child. Richard looked down upon him; but he was kind, as a generous-tempered boy could not fail to be, to one younger and weaker than himself. He was so much kinder than Lothaire, that Carloman was fast growing very fond of him, and looked up to his strength and courage as something noble and marvellous.

It was very different with Lothaire, the person from whom, above all others, Richard would have most expected to meet with affection, as his father's godson, a relationship which in those times was thought almost as near as **kindred by blood**. Lothaire had been brought up by an indulgent mother, and by courtiers who never ceased flattering him, as the heir to the crown, and he had learnt to think that to give way to his naturally imperious and violent disposition was the way to prove his power and assert his rank. He had always had his own way, and nothing had ever been done to **check his faults**; somewhat weakly health had made him fretful and timid; and a latent consciousness of this fearfulness made him all the more cruel, sometimes because he was frightened, sometimes because he fancied it manly.

Part Two

Warning for sensitive readers: Lothaire's cruelty to animals is described very clearly in this passage, and you may wish to skip the details. The short version: he is angry at a falcon because it pecked him, and he plans to do something dreadful to it. Richard gets in the way, and his face is burned. The boys get into a fist fight, and the falcon flies away.

[Lothaire] treated his little brother in a way which in these times boys would call bullying; and, as no one ever dared to oppose the King's eldest son, it was pretty much the same with every one else, except now and then some [animal], and then all Lothaire's cruelty was shown. When his horse kicked, and ended by throwing him, he stood by, and caused it to be beaten till the poor creature's back streamed with blood; when his dog bit his hand in trying to seize the meat with which he was teasing it, he insisted on having it killed, and it was worse still when a **falcon** pecked one of his fingers. It really hurt him a good deal, and, in a furious rage, he caused two nails to be heated red hot in the fire, intending to have them thrust into the poor bird's eyes.

"I will not have it done!" exclaimed Richard, expecting to be obeyed as he was at home; but Lothaire only laughed scornfully, saying, "Do you think you are master here, Sir Pirate?"

"I will not have it done!" repeated Richard. "Shame on you, shame on you, for thinking of such an unkingly deed."

"Shame on me! Do you know to whom you speak, Master Savage?" cried Lothaire, red with passion.

"I know who is the savage now!" said Richard. "Hold!" to the servant who was bringing the red-hot irons in a pair of tongs.

"Hold?" exclaimed Lothaire. "No one commands here but I and my father. Go on, Charlot–where is the bird? Keep her fast, Giles."

"Osmond. You I can command–"

"Come away, my Lord," said Osmond, interrupting Richard's order before it was issued. "We have no right to interfere here, and cannot hinder it. Come away from such a foul sight."

"Shame on you too, Osmond, to let such a deed be done without hindering it!" exclaimed Richard, breaking from him, and rushing on the man who carried the hot irons. The French servants were not very willing to exert their strength against the Duke of Normandy, and Richard's onset, taking the man by surprise, made him drop the tongs. Lothaire, both afraid and enraged, caught them up as a weapon of defence, and, hardly knowing what he did, struck full at Richard's face with the hot iron. Happily it missed his eye, and the heat had a little **abated**; but, as it touched his cheek, it burnt him sufficiently to cause considerable pain. With a cry of passion, he flew at Lothaire, shook him with all his might, and ended by throwing him at his length on the pavement. But this was the last of Richard's exploits, for he was at the same moment captured by his Squire, and borne off, struggling and kicking as if Osmond had been his greatest foe; but the young Norman's arms were like iron round him; and he gave over his resistance sooner, because at that moment a whirring flapping sound was heard, and the poor hawk rose high, higher, over their heads in ever lessening circles, far away from her enemies. The servant who held her, had relaxed his grasp in the **consternation** caused by Lothaire's fall, and she was mounting up and up, spying, it might be, her way to her native rocks in Iceland, with the yellow eyes which Richard had saved.

"Safe! safe!" cried Richard, joyfully, ceasing his struggles. "Oh, how glad I am! That young villain should never have hurt her. Put me down, Osmond, what are you doing with me?"

"Saving you from your–no, I cannot call it folly,–I would hardly have had you stand still to see such–but let me see your face."

"It is nothing. I don't care now the hawk is safe," said Richard, though he could hardly keep his lips in order, and was obliged to wink very hard with his eyes to keep the tears out, now that he had **leisure to feel the smarting**; but it would have been far beneath a Northman to complain, and he stood bearing it gallantly, and pinching his fingers tightly together, while Osmond knelt down to examine the hurt. " 'Tis not much," said he, talking to himself, "half bruise, half burn–I wish my grandmother was here–however, it can't last long! 'Tis right, you bear it like a little **Berserkar**, and it is no bad thing that you should have a scar to show, that they may not be able to say you did *all* the damage."

"Will it always leave a mark?" said Richard. "I am afraid they will call me Richard of the scarred cheek, when we get back to Normandy."

"Never mind, if they do–it will not be a mark to be ashamed of, even if it does last, which I do not believe it will."

"Oh, no, I am so glad the gallant falcon is out of his reach!" replied Richard, in a somewhat quivering voice.

"Does it smart much? Well, come and bathe it with cold water–or shall I take you to one of the Queen's women?"

"No–the water," said Richard, and to the fountain in the court they went; but Osmond had only just begun to splash the cheek with the half-frozen water, with a sort of rough kindness, afraid at once of teaching the Duke to be **effeminate**, and of not being as tender to him as Dame Astrida would have wished, when a messenger came in haste from the King, commanding the presence of the Duke of Normandy and his Squire.

Part Three

Lothaire was standing between his father and mother on their throne-like seat, leaning against the Queen, who had her arm round him; his face was red and glazed with tears, and he still shook with subsiding sobs. It was evident he was just recovering from a passionate crying fit.

"How is this?" began the King, as Richard entered. "What means this conduct, my Lord of Normandy? Know you what you have done in striking the heir of France? I might imprison you this instant in a dungeon where you would never see the light of day."

"Then Bernard de Harcourt would come and set me free," fearlessly answered Richard.

"Do you bandy words with me, child? Ask Prince Lothaire's pardon instantly, or you shall rue it."

"I have done nothing to ask his pardon for. It would have been cruel and cowardly in me to let him put out the poor hawk's eyes," said Richard, with a Northman's stern contempt for pain, disdaining to mention his own burnt cheek, which indeed the King might have seen plainly enough.

"Hawk's eyes!" repeated the King. "Speak the truth, Sir Duke; do not add **slander** to your other faults."

"I have spoken the truth–I always speak it!" cried Richard. "Whoever says otherwise lies in his throat."

Osmond here hastily interfered, and desired permission to tell the whole story. The hawk was a valuable bird, and Louis's face darkened when he heard what Lothaire had purposed, for the Prince had, in telling his own story, made it appear that Richard had been the aggressor by insisting on letting the falcon fly. Osmond finished by pointing to the mark on Richard's cheek, so evidently a burn, as to be proof that hot iron had played a part in the matter. The King looked at one of his own Squires and asked his account, and he with some hesitation could not but reply that it was as the young **Sieur de Centeville** had said. Thereupon Louis angrily reproved his own people for having assisted the Prince in trying to injure the hawk, called for the chief falconer, rated him for not better attending to his birds, and went forth with him to see if the hawk could yet be recaptured, leaving the two boys neither punished nor pardoned.

"So you have escaped for this once," said Gerberge, coldly, to Richard; "you had better beware another time. Come with me, my poor darling Lothaire." She led her son away to her own apartments, and the French Squires began to grumble to each other complaints of the impossibility of pleasing their Lords, since, if they contradicted Prince Lothaire, he was so spiteful that he was sure to set the Queen against them, and that was far worse in the end than the King's displeasure. Osmond, in the meantime, took Richard to re-commence bathing his face, and presently Carloman ran out to pity him, wonder at him for not crying, and say he was glad the poor hawk had escaped.

Part Four

The cheek continued inflamed and painful for some time, and there was a deep scar long after the pain had ceased, but Richard thought little of it after the first, and would have scorned to bear ill-will to Lothaire for the injury.

Lothaire left off taunting Richard with his Norman accent, and calling him a "young Sea-king." He had felt his strength, and was afraid of him; but he did not like him the better–he never played with him willingly–scowled, and looked dark and jealous, if his father, or if any of the great nobles took the least notice of the little Duke, and whenever he was out of hearing, talked against him with all his natural spitefulness.

Richard liked Lothaire quite as little, contemning almost equally his cowardly ways and his imperious disposition. Since he had been Duke, Richard had been somewhat inclined to grow imperious himself, though always kept under restraint by Fru Astrida's good training, and Count Bernard's authority, and his whole generous nature would have revolted against treating Alberic, or indeed his **meanest** vassal, as Lothaire used the unfortunate children who were his playfellows. Perhaps this made him look on with great horror at the tyranny which Lothaire exercised; at any rate he learnt to abhor it more, and to make many resolutions against ordering people about uncivilly when once he should be in Normandy again. He often interfered to protect **the**

poor boys, and generally with success, for the Prince was afraid of provoking such another shake as Richard had once given him, and though he generally repaid himself on his victim in the end, he yielded for the time.

Narration and Discussion

Why does Richard call hurting an animal an "unkingly deed?" Was Richard brave or foolish to interfere with Lothaire's cruelty?

What made King Louis change his mind about punishing Richard?

Creative narration: Tell back the events of this chapter from the point of view of a) Queen Gerberge, b) Osmond, or c) the falcon.

For further thought: How is Richard beginning to change his thinking about how princes, kings, and dukes should act? Here is a Bible verse about righteous kings:

> When the righteous are in authority, the people rejoice: but when the wicked beareth rule, the people mourn. (Proverbs 29:2)

Can you think of any other stories about very good or very bad rulers?

Chapter Seven: Captors and Captive (Part 2)

Introduction

When: The same year and into the next, ending in late spring

Where: Laon

The winter goes by and things continue on without much change, but when Count Hugh visits at Easter, he warns Osmond to watch out for trouble. At the Whitsunday feast (several weeks later), one of the guests is Count Arnulf, the murderer of Duke William. When Richard refuses to attend the dinner, trouble follows.

Vocabulary

forbear: refrain from doing something; stop before going too far

in his prosperity: safety, well-being

vigilant: unwavering, constant

"his own loyalty and forbearance": his belief that a subject should be loyal to his King, no matter whether he likes or approves of that King or not

the feeble and degenerate race of Charlemagne: Charlemagne was a great king, but his descendants (such as Louis) seemed to be weak and corrupt.

perceive: notice

reproved: corrected, scolded

you must one day be friends with them as your father has been with me: Yonge is foreshadowing a bit here, as Richard will grow up to marry Eumacette

tranquillity: peace

intelligence: news, information

token of mischief: sign of trouble

quitted: left

Whitsuntide: the seventh Sunday after Easter, also known as Pentecost

will take it amiss: won't like it

challenge [someone] to single combat: dare the person to have a sword fight

fast: go hungry, not eat

furbishing: polishing

fray: fight

designs: plans, plots

air of gratified malice: nasty smug grin

People, Places, Events

Oise: a river that flows through Belgium and France

Reading

Part One

Carloman, whom Richard often saved from his brother's unkindness, clung closer and closer to him, went with him everywhere, tried to do all he did, grew very fond of Osmond, and liked nothing better than to sit by Richard in some wide window-seat, in the evening, after supper, and listen to Richard's version of some of Fru Astrida's favourite tales, or hear the never-ending history of sports at Centeville, or at Rollo's Tower, or settle what great things they would both do when they were grown up, and Richard was ruling Normandy–perhaps go to the Holy Land together, and slaughter an unheard-of host of giants and dragons on the way. In the meantime, however, poor Carloman gave small promise of being able to perform great exploits, for he was very small for his age and often ailing; soon tired, and never able to bear much rough play. Richard, who had never had any reason to learn to **forbear**, did not at first understand this, and made Carloman cry several times with his roughness and violence, but this always vexed him so much that he grew careful to avoid such things for the future, and gradually learnt to treat his poor little weakly friend with a gentleness and patience at which Osmond used to marvel, and which he would hardly have been taught **in his prosperity** at home.

Between Carloman and Osmond he was thus tolerably happy at Laon, but he missed his own dear friends, and the loving greetings of his vassals, and longed earnestly to be at Rouen, asking Osmond almost every night when they should go back, to which Osmond could only answer that he must pray that Heaven would be pleased to bring them home safely.

Osmond, in the meantime, kept a **vigilant** watch for anything that might seem to threaten danger to his Lord; but at present there was no token of any evil being intended; the only point in which Louis did not seem to be fulfilling his promises to the Normans was, that no preparations were made for attacking the Count of Flanders.

Part Two

At Easter the court was visited by Hugh the White, the great Count of Paris, the most powerful man in France, and who was only prevented by **his own loyalty and forbearance**, from taking the crown from **the feeble and degenerate race of Charlemagne.** He had been a firm friend of [Richard's father], and Osmond remarked how, on his arrival, the King took care to bring Richard forward, talk of him affectionately, and caress him almost as much as he had done at Rouen [*omission*]. He soon asked about the scar which the burn had left, and the King was obliged to answer hastily, it was an accident, a disaster that had chanced in a boyish quarrel. Louis, in fact, was uneasy, and appeared to be watching the Count of Paris the whole time of his visit, so as to prevent him from having any conversation in private with the other great vassals assembled at the court. Hugh did not seem to **perceive** this, and acted as if he was entirely at his ease, but at the same time he watched his opportunity. One evening, after supper, he came up to the window where Richard and Carloman were, as usual, deep in story telling; he sat down on the stone seat, and taking Richard on his knee, he asked if he had any greetings for the Count de Harcourt.

How Richard's face lighted up! "Oh, Sir," he cried, "are you going to Normandy?"

"Not yet, my boy, but it may be that I may have to meet old Harcourt at the Elm of Gisors."

"Oh, if I was but going with you."

"I wish I could take you, but it would scarcely do for me to steal the heir of Normandy. What shall I tell him?"

"Tell him," whispered Richard, edging himself close to the Count, and trying to reach his ear, "tell him that I am sorry, now, that I was sullen when he **reproved** me. I know he was right. And, sir, if he brings with him a certain huntsman with a long hooked nose, whose name is Walter, tell him I am sorry I used to order him about so unkindly. And tell him to bear my greetings to Fru Astrida and Sir Eric, and to Alberic."

"Shall I tell him how you have marked your face?"

"No," said Richard, "he would think me a baby to care about such a thing as that!"

The Count asked how it happened, and Richard told the story, for he felt as if he could tell the kind Count anything–it was almost like that last evening that he had sat on his father's knee. Hugh ended by putting his arm round him, and saying, "Well, my little Duke, I am as glad as you are the gallant bird is safe–it will be a tale for my own little Hugh and Eumacette at home–and **you must one day be friends with them as your father has been with me**. And now, do you think your Squire could come to my chamber late this evening when the household is at rest?"

Richard undertook that Osmond should do so, and the Count, setting him down again, returned to the dais. Osmond, before going to the Count that evening, ordered Sybald to come and guard the Duke's door. It was a long conference, for Hugh had come to Laon chiefly for the purpose of seeing how it went with his friend's son, and was anxious to know what Osmond thought of the matter. They agreed that at present there did not seem to be any evil intended, and that it rather appeared as if Louis wished only to keep him as a hostage for the **tranquillity** of the borders of Normandy; but Hugh advised that Osmond should maintain a careful watch, and send **intelligence** to him on the first **token of mischief**.

Part Three

Spoiler for sensitive readers: The Norman grooms, Sybald and Henry, are killed (this takes place offstage).

The next morning the Count of Paris **quitted** Laon, and everything went on in the usual course till the feast of **Whitsuntide**, when there was always a great display of splendour at the French court. The crown vassals generally came to pay their duty and go with the King to Church; and there was a state banquet, at which the King and Queen wore their crowns, and every one sat in great magnificence according to their rank.

The grand procession to Church was over. Richard had walked with Carloman, the Prince richly dressed in blue, embroidered with golden fleur-de-lys, and Richard in scarlet, with a gold Cross on his breast. The beautiful service was over, they had returned to the Castle, and there the Seneschal was marshalling the goodly and noble company to the banquet, when horses' feet were heard at the gate announcing some fresh arrival. The Seneschal went to receive the guests, and presently was heard ushering in the noble Prince, Arnulf, Count of Flanders.

Richard's face became pale–he turned from Carloman by whose side he had been standing, and walked straight out of the hall and up the stairs, closely followed by Osmond. In a few minutes there was a knock at the door of his chamber, and a French Knight stood there saying, "Comes not the Duke to the banquet?"

"No," answered Osmond: "he eats not with the slayer of his father."

"The King **will take it amiss**; for the sake of the child you had better beware," said the Frenchman, hesitating.

"He had better beware himself," exclaimed Osmond, indignantly, "how he brings the treacherous murderer of William Longsword into the presence of a free-born Norman, unless he would see him slain where he stands. Were it not for the boy, I would **challenge** the traitor this instant to **single combat**."

"Well, I can scarce blame you," said the Knight, "but you had best have a care how you tread. Farewell."

Richard had hardly time to express his indignation, and his wishes that he was a man, before another message came through a groom of Lothaire's train, that the Duke must **fast**, if he would not consent to feast with the rest.

"Tell Prince Lothaire," replied Richard, "that I am not such a glutton as he–I had rather fast than be choked with eating with Arnulf."

All the rest of the day, Richard remained in his own chamber, resolved not to run the risk of meeting with Arnulf. The Squire remained with him, in this voluntary imprisonment, and they occupied themselves, as best they could, with **furbishing** Osmond's armour, and helping each other out in repeating some of the Sagas. They once heard a great uproar in the court, and both were very anxious to learn its cause, but they did not know it till late in the afternoon.

Carloman crept up to them– "Here I am at last!" he exclaimed. "Here, Richard, I have brought you some bread, as you had no dinner: it was all I could bring. I saved it under the table lest Lothaire should see it."

Richard thanked Carloman with all his heart, and being very hungry was glad to share the bread with Osmond. He asked how long the wicked Count was going to stay, and rejoiced to hear he was going away the next morning, and the King was going with him.

"What was that great noise in the court?" asked Richard.

"I scarcely like to tell you," returned Carloman.

Richard, however, begged to hear, and Carloman was obliged to tell that the two Norman grooms, Sybald and Henry, had quarrelled with the Flemings [who had come with Arnulf]; there had been a **fray**, which had ended in the death of three Flemings, a Frank, and of Sybald himself–And where was Henry? Alas! there was more ill news–the King had sentenced Henry to die, and he had been hanged immediately.

Dark with anger and sorrow grew young Richard's face; he had been fond of his two Norman attendants, he trusted to their attachment, and he would have wept for their loss even if it had happened in any other way; but now, when it had been caused by their enmity to his father's foes, the Flemings,–when one had fallen overwhelmed by numbers, and the other been condemned hastily, cruelly, unjustly, it was too much, and he almost choked with grief and indignation. Why had he not been there, to claim Henry as his own vassal, and if he could not save him, at least bid him farewell? Then he would have broken out in angry threats, but he felt his own helplessness, and was ashamed, and he could only shed tears of passionate grief, refusing all Carloman's attempts to comfort him.

Osmond was even more concerned; he valued the two Normans extremely for their courage and faithfulness, and had relied on sending intelligence by their means to Rouen, in case of need. It appeared to him as if the first opportunity had been seized of removing these protectors from the little Duke, and as if the **designs**, whatever they might be, which had been formed against him, were about to take effect. He had little doubt that his own turn would be the next; but he was resolved to endure anything, rather than give the smallest opportunity of removing him, to bear even insults with patience, and to remember that in his care rested the sole hope of safety for his charge.

Part Four

That danger was fast gathering around them became more evident every day, especially after the King and Arnulf had gone away together. It was very hot weather, and Richard began to weary after the broad cool river at Rouen, where he used to bathe last summer; and one evening he persuaded his Squire to go down with him to the **Oise**, which flowed along some meadow ground about a quarter of a mile from the Castle; but they had hardly set forth before three or four attendants came running after them, with express orders from the Queen that they should return immediately. They obeyed, and found her standing in the Castle hall, looking greatly incensed.

"What means this?" she asked, angrily. "Knew you not that the King has left commands that the Duke quits not the Castle in his absence?"

"I was only going as far as the river–" began Richard, but Gerberge cut him short. "Silence, child–I will hear no excuses." [Then she said to Osmond], "Perhaps you think, Sieur de Centeville, that you may take liberties in the King's absence, but I tell you that if you are found without the walls again, it shall be at your peril; aye, and his! I'll have those haughty eyes put out, if you disobey!"

She turned away, and Lothaire looked at them with his **air of gratified malice**. "You will not lord it over your betters much longer, young pirate!" said he, as he followed his mother, afraid to stay to meet the anger he might have excited by the taunt he could not deny himself the pleasure of making; but Richard, who, six months ago could not brook a slight disappointment or opposition, had, in his present life of restraint, danger, and vexation, learnt to curb the first outbreak of temper, and to bear patiently instead of breaking out into passion and threats, and now his only thought was of his beloved Squire.

"Oh, Osmond! Osmond!" he exclaimed, "they shall not hurt you. I will never go out again. I will never speak another hasty word. I will never affront the Prince, if they will but leave you with me!"

Narration and Discussion

Having dinner with Count Arnulf seems like too much to ask, even for the new-and-improved Duke Richard. Should he have swallowed his anger and hate, and joined the party?

"Hugh advised that Osmond should maintain a careful watch, and send intelligence to him on the first token of mischief." Do you think now would be a good time for that?

Creative narration #1: Count Hugh said, "Well, my little Duke, I am as glad as you are the gallant bird is safe–it will be a tale for my own little Hugh and Eumacette at home." Pretend you are Count Hugh back at home, telling his children about what he has been doing.

Creative narration #2: Act out the last scene, when Richard and Osmond come back from swimming.

For further thought: "Richard, who, six months ago could not brook a slight disappointment or opposition, had, in his present life of restraint, danger, and vexation, learnt to curb the first outbreak of temper, and to bear patiently instead of breaking out into passion and threats." Living through hard things can teach us to be braver, kinder, or more patient. Can you think of any other stories where someone went through difficulties that helped them grow stronger, or to have greater faith in God?

Chapter Eight: A Bundle of Straw (Part 1)

Introduction

When: Summer of the year 944 A.D.

Settings: The castle of Laon; later, the country between Laon and Normandy

When Richard becomes ill (could it be poison?), Osmond decides it is time to escape from Laon, once and for all.

Vocabulary

alms: money given to poor people

pilgrim: traveller, especially one journeying for religious reasons

scrip: bag

girdle: belt

obeisances: bows

sup: eat

the chase: hunting animals

disappointed of his game: had not caught anything

scourge: whip

thong: leather strap

sanctity: holiness

gain an interview with Osmond: get a chance to speak with him

evil tidings: bad news

expire: die

assiduously: carefully

loath: unwilling

provisions: food

wallet: bag

what recked he: what did he care

Reading

Part One

It was a fine summer evening, and Richard and Carloman were playing at ball on the steps of the Castle-gate, when a voice was heard from beneath, begging for "**alms** from the noble Princes in the name of the blessed Virgin," and the two boys saw a **pilgrim** standing at the gate, wrapped in a long robe of serge, with a staff in his hand, surmounted by a Cross, a **scrip** at his girdle, and a broad shady hat, which he had taken off, as he stood, making low **obeisances**, and asking charity.

"Come in, holy pilgrim," said Carloman. "It is late, and you shall **sup** and rest here to-night."

"Blessings from Heaven light on you, noble Prince," replied the pilgrim, and at that moment Richard shouted joyfully, "A Norman, a Norman! 'tis my own dear speech! Oh, are you not from Normandy? Osmond, Osmond! He comes from home!"

"My Lord! my own Lord!" exclaimed the pilgrim, and, kneeling on one knee at the foot of the steps, he kissed the hand which his young Duke held out to him– "This is joy unlooked for!"

"Walter!–Walter, the huntsman!" cried Richard. "Is it you? Oh, how is Fru Astrida, and all at home?"

"Well, my Lord, and wearying to know how it is with you–" began Walter–but a very different tone exclaimed from behind the pilgrim, "What is all this? Who is stopping my way? What! Richard would be King, and more, would he? More insolence!" It was Lothaire, returning with his attendants from **the chase**, in by no means an amiable mood, for he had been **disappointed of his game**.

"He is a Norman–a vassal of Richard's own," said Carloman.

"A Norman, is he? I thought we had got rid of the robbers! We want no robbers here! **Scourge** him soundly, Perron, and teach him how to stop my way!"

"He is a pilgrim, my Lord," suggested one of the followers.

"I care not; I'll have no Normans here, coming spying in disguise. Scourge him, I say, dog that he is! Away with him! A spy, a spy!"

"No Norman is scourged in my sight!" said Richard, darting forwards, and throwing himself between Walter and the woodsman, who was preparing to obey Lothaire, just in time to receive on his own bare neck the sharp, cutting leather **thong**, which raised a long red streak along its course. Lothaire laughed.

"My Lord Duke! What have you done? Oh, leavc me–this befits you not!" cried Walter, extremely distressed; but Richard had caught hold of the whip, and called out, "Away, away! run! haste, haste!" and the words were repeated at once by Osmond, Carloman, and many of the French, who, though afraid to disobey the Prince, were unwilling to violate the **sanctity** of a pilgrim's person; and the Norman, seeing there was no help for it, obeyed: the French made way for him and he effected his escape; while Lothaire, after a great deal of storming and raging, went up to his mother to triumph in the cleverness with which he had detected a Norman spy in disguise.

Part Two

Lothaire was not far wrong; Walter had really come to satisfy himself as to the safety of the little Duke, and try to **gain an interview with Osmond**. In the latter purpose he failed, though he lingered in the neighbourhood of Laon for several days; for Osmond never left the Duke for an instant, and he was, as has been shown, a close prisoner, in all but the name, within the walls of the Castle. The pilgrim had, however, the opportunity of picking up tidings which made him perceive the true state of things: he learnt the deaths of Sybald and Henry, the alliance between the King and Arnulf, and the restraint and harshness with which the Duke was treated; and [with this news] he went in haste to Normandy.

Soon after his arrival, a three days' fast was observed throughout the dukedom, and in every church, from the Cathedral of Bayeux to the smallest [*omission*] village shrine, crowds of worshippers were kneeling, imploring, many of them with tears, that God would look on them in His mercy, restore to them their Prince, and deliver the child out of the hands of his enemies. How earnest and sorrowful were the prayers offered at Centeville may well be imagined; and at Montémar sur Epte the anxiety was scarcely less. Indeed, from the time the **evil tidings** arrived, Alberic grew so restless and unhappy, and so anxious to do something, that at last his mother set out with him on a pilgrimage to the Abbey of Jumièges, to pray for the rescue of his dear little Duke.

Part Three

In the meantime, Louis had sent notice to Laon that he should return home in a week's time; and Richard rejoiced at the prospect, for the King had always been less unkind to him than the Queen, and he hoped to be released from his captivity within the Castle. Just at this time he became very unwell; it might have been only the effect of the life of unwonted confinement which he had lately led that was beginning to tell on his health; but, after being heavy and uncomfortable for a day or two, without knowing what was the matter with him, he was one night attacked with high fever.

Osmond was dreadfully alarmed, knowing nothing at all of the treatment of illness, and, what was worse, fully persuaded that the poor child had been poisoned, and therefore resolved not to call any assistance; he hung over him all night, expecting each moment to see him **expire**–ready to tear his hair with despair and fury, and yet obliged to restrain himself to the utmost quietness and gentleness, to soothe the suffering of the sick child.

Through that night, Richard either tossed about on his narrow bed, or, when his restlessness desired the change, sat, leaning his aching head on Osmond's breast, too oppressed and miserable to speak or think. When the day dawned on them, and he was still too ill to leave the room, messengers were sent for him, and Osmond could no longer conceal the fact of his sickness, but parleyed at the door, keeping out every one he could, and refusing all offers of attendance. He would not even admit Carloman, though Richard, hearing his voice, begged to see him; and when a proposal was sent from the Queen that a skillful old nurse should visit and prescribe for the patient, he refused with all his might, and when he had shut the door, walked up and down, muttering, "Aye, aye [*omission*], she is coming to finish what she has begun!"

All that day and the next, Richard continued very ill, and Osmond waited on him very **assiduously**, never closing his eyes for a moment, but constantly telling his beads whenever the boy did not require his attendance.

At last Richard fell asleep, slept long and soundly for some hours, and waked much better. Osmond was in a transport of joy: "Thanks to Heaven, they shall fail for this time and they shall never have another chance! May Heaven be with us still!" Richard was too weak and weary to ask what he meant, and for the next few days Osmond watched him with the utmost care. As for food, now that Richard could eat again, Osmond would not hear of his touching what was sent for him from the royal table, but always went down himself to procure food in the kitchen, where he said he had a friend among the cooks, who would, he thought, scarcely poison him intentionally. When Richard was able to cross the room, he insisted on his always fastening the door with his dagger, and never opening to any summons but his own, not even Prince Carloman's. Richard wondered, but he was obliged to obey; and he knew enough of the perils around him to perceive the reasonableness of Osmond's caution.

Part Four

Thus several days had passed, the King had returned, and Richard was so much recovered, that he had become very anxious to be allowed to go down stairs again, instead of remaining shut up there; but still Osmond would not consent, though Richard had done nothing all day but walk round the room, to show how strong he was.

"Now, my Lord, guard the door–take care," said Osmond; "you have no loss to-day, for the King has brought home Herluin of Montreuil, whom you would be almost as **loath** to meet as the Fleming. And tell your beads while I am gone, that the Saints may bring us out of our peril."

Osmond was absent nearly half an hour, and, when he returned, brought on his shoulders a huge bundle of straw. "What is this for?" exclaimed Richard. "I wanted my supper, and you have brought straw!"

"Here is your supper," said Osmond, throwing down the straw, and producing a bag with some bread and meat. "What should you say, my Lord, if we should sup in Normandy tomorrow night?"

"In Normandy!" cried Richard, springing up and clapping his hands. "In Normandy! Oh, Osmond, did you say in Normandy? Shall we, shall we really? Oh, joy! joy! Is Count Bernard come? Will the King let us go?"

"Hush! hush, sir! It must be our own doing; it will all fail if you are not silent and prudent, and we shall be undone."

"I will do anything to get home again!"

"Eat first," said Osmond.

"But what are you going to do? I will not be as foolish as I was when you tried to get me safe out of Rollo's tower. But I should like to wish Carloman farewell."

"That must not be," said Osmond; "we should not have time to escape, if they did not still believe you very ill in bed."

"I am sorry not to wish Carloman good-bye," repeated Richard; "but we shall see Fru Astrida again, and Sir Eric; and Alberic must come back! Oh, do let us go! O Normandy, dear Normandy!"

Part Five

Richard could hardly eat for excitement, while Osmond hastily made his arrangements, girding on his sword, and giving Richard his dagger to put into his belt. He placed the remainder of the **provisions** in his **wallet**, threw a thick purple cloth mantle over the Duke, and then desired him to lie down on the straw which he had brought in. "I shall hide you in it," he said, "and carry you through the hall, as if I was going to feed my horse."

"Oh, they will never guess!" cried Richard, laughing. "I will be quite still–I will make no noise–I will hold my breath."

"Yes, mind you do not move hand or foot, or rustle the straw. It is no play–it is life or death," said Osmond, as he disposed the straw round the little boy. "There, can you breathe?"

"Yes," said Richard's voice from the midst. "Am I quite hidden?"

"Entirely. Now, remember, whatever happens, do not move. May Heaven protect us! Now, the Saints be with us!"

Richard, from the interior of the bundle heard Osmond set open the door; then he felt himself raised from the ground; Osmond was carrying him along down the stairs, the ends of the straw crushing and sweeping against the wall. The only way to the outer door was through the hall, and here was the danger. Richard heard voices, steps, loud singing and laughter, as if feasting was going on; then some one said, "Tending your horse, Sieur de Centeville?"

"Yes," Osmond made answer. "You know, since we lost our

grooms, the poor black would come off badly, did I not attend to him."

Presently came Carloman's voice: "Oh, Osmond de Centeville! is Richard better?"

"He is better, my Lord, I thank you, but hardly yet out of danger."

"Oh, I wish he was well! And when will you let me come to him, Osmond? Indeed, I would sit quiet, and not disturb him."

"It may not be yet, my Lord, though the Duke loves you well–he told me so but now."

"Did he? Oh, tell him I love him very much–better than anyone here–and it is very dull without him. Tell him so, Osmond."

Richard could hardly help calling out to his dear little Carloman; but he remembered the peril of Osmond's eyes and the Queen's threat, and held his peace, with some vague notion that some day he would make Carloman King of France. In the meantime, half stifled with the straw, he felt himself carried on, down the steps, across the court; and then he knew, from the darkness and the changed sound of Osmond's tread, that they were in the stable. Osmond laid him carefully down, and whispered– "All right so far. You can breathe?"

"Not well. Can't you let me out?"

"Not yet–not for worlds. Now tell me if I put you face downwards, for I cannot see."

He laid the living heap of straw across the saddle, bound it on, then led out the horse, gazing round cautiously as he did so; but the whole of the people of the Castle were feasting, and there was no one to watch the gates. Richard heard the hollow sound of the hoofs, as the drawbridge was crossed, and knew that he was free; but still Osmond held his arm over him, and would not let him move, for some distance.

Part Six

Then, just as Richard felt as if he could endure the stifling of the straw, and his uncomfortable position, not a moment longer, Osmond stopped the horse, took him down, laid him on the grass, and released him. He gazed around; they were in a little wood; evening twilight was just coming on, and the birds sang sweetly.

"Free! free!–this is freedom!" cried Richard, leaping up in the delicious cool evening breeze; "the Queen and Lothaire, and that grim room, all far behind."

"Not so far yet," said Osmond; "you must not call yourself safe till the Epte is between us and them. Into the saddle, my Lord; we must ride for our lives."

Osmond helped the Duke to mount, and sprang to the saddle behind him, set spurs to the horse, and rode on at a quick rate, though not at full speed, as he wished to spare the horse. The twilight faded, the stars came out, and still he rode, his arm round the child, who, as night advanced, grew weary, and often sunk into a sort of half doze, conscious all the time of the trot of the horse. But each step was taking him further from Queen Gerberge, and nearer to Normandy; and **what recked he** of weariness?

Narration and Discussion

Why couldn't Osmond call a doctor to help Richard?

How was this escape different from the time Richard's friends tried to get him out of the castle at Rouen?

For further thought: What does the Bible tell us about praying when we are sick or in danger? Do you think maybe God put the "bundle of straw" idea into Osmond's mind?

Creative narration: Richard's escape might be fun to act out. (Just be careful when wrapping people up or carrying them!)

For further exploration: What do you do at your house when someone is sick? Young students might enjoy *Just a Little Sick* by Mercer Mayer; *Tell Me a Mitzi* by Lore Segal (everybody in Mitzi's family gets sick, but Grandma shows up to help); or *Get Well, Good Knight* by Shelley Moore Thomas (parental caution: involves a pot of "scaly snail-y soup" made by a wizard). Our children's favourite was "Sick in Bed" in *Amanda Pig On Her Own* by Jean Van Leeuwen, which added "My eyes are all juicy" and "Rest, my sweet potato" to our family phrase book. (None of these stories involve serious illness or injury.)

Chapter Eight: A Bundle of Straw (Part 2)

Introduction

When: The same day

Where: The French countryside between Laon and Normandy; Montémar (Alberic's castle)

The journey is a hard one, but the two escapees finally reach safety in Montémar.

Vocabulary

mended his pace: went a little faster

barter: trade

yonder stout palfrey: that strong horse

chaffer: haggle about the price

sagacity: wisdom

pursuit: chase

fatigue: tiredness

forded: crossed (by someone else before them)

I doubt me: I'm pretty sure

imprudence: lack of care

the bar-tailed hawk: the falcon Richard had asked Alberic to care for

pennon: flag, banner

relish: enjoyment

People, Places, Events

Dame Yolande Montémar: Alberic's mother

King Harald Horrid-locks: the king of Norway who took a vow not to cut his hair (see *Viking Tales*, "Gyda's Saucy Message")

Reading

Part One

On–on; the stars grew pale again, and the first pink light of dawn showed in the eastern sky; the sun rose, mounted higher and higher, and the day grew hotter; the horse went more slowly, stumbled, and though Osmond halted and loosed the girth, he only **mended his pace** for a little while.

Osmond looked grievously perplexed; but they had not gone much further before a party of merchants came in sight, winding their way with a long train of loaded mules, and stout men to guard them, across the plains, like an eastern caravan in the desert. They gazed in surprise at the tall young Norman holding the child upon the worn-out war-horse.

"Sir merchant," said Osmond to the first, "see you this steed? Better horse never was ridden; but he is sorely spent, and we must make speed. Let me **barter** him with you for **yonder stout palfrey**. He is worth twice as much, but I cannot stop to **chaffer**–aye or no at once."

The merchant, seeing the value of Osmond's gallant black, accepted the offer; and Osmond removing his saddle, and placing Richard on his new steed, again mounted, and on they went through the country which Osmond's eye had marked with the **sagacity** men acquire by living in wild, unsettled places. The great marshes were now far less dangerous than in the winter, and they safely crossed them. There had, as yet, been no **pursuit**, and Osmond's only fear was for his little charge, who, not having recovered his full strength since his illness, began to suffer greatly from **fatigue** in the heat of that broiling summer day, and leant against Osmond patiently, but very wearily, without moving or looking up.

He scarcely revived when the sun went down, and a cool breeze sprang up, which much refreshed Osmond himself; and still more did it refresh the Squire to see, at length, winding through the green pastures, a blue river, on the opposite bank of which rose a high rocky mound, bearing a castle with many a turret and battlement.

"The Epte! the Epte! There is Normandy, sir! Look up, and see your own dukedom."

"Normandy!" cried Richard, sitting upright. "Oh, my own home!"

Still the Epte was wide and deep, and the peril was not yet ended. Osmond looked anxiously, and rejoiced to see marks of cattle, as if it had been **forded**. "We must try it," he said, and dismounting, he waded in, leading the horse, and firmly holding Richard in the saddle. Deep they went; the water rose to Richard's feet, then to the horse's neck; then the horse was swimming, and Osmond too, still keeping his firm hold; then there was ground again, the force of the current was less, and they were gaining the bank. At that instant, however, they perceived two men aiming at them with cross-bows from the castle, and another standing on the bank above them, who called out, "Hold! None pass the ford of Montémar without permission of the noble Dame Yolande."

"Ha! Bertrand the Seneschal, is that you?" returned Osmond. "Who calls me by my name?" replied the Seneschal. "It is I, Osmond de Centeville. Open your gates quickly, Sir Seneschal; for here is the Duke, sorely in need of rest and refreshment."

"The Duke!" exclaimed Bertrand, hurrying down to the landing-place, and throwing off his cap. "The Duke! the Duke!" rang out the shout from the men-at-arms on the battlements above and in an instant more Osmond had led the horse up from the water, and was exclaiming, "Look up, my Lord, look up! You are in your own dukedom again, and this is Alberic's castle."

Part Two

"Welcome, indeed, most noble Lord Duke! Blessings on the day!" cried the Seneschal. "What joy for my Lady and my young Lord!"

"He is sorely weary," said Osmond, looking anxiously at Richard, who, even at the welcome cries that showed so plainly that he was in his own Normandy, scarcely raised himself or spoke. "He had been very sick ere I brought him away. **I doubt me** they sought to poison him, and I vowed not to tarry at Laon another hour after he was fit to move. But cheer up, my Lord; you are safe and free now, and here is the good Dame de Montémar to tend you, far better than a rude Squire like me."

"Alas, no!" said the Seneschal; "our Dame is gone with young Alberic on a pilgrimage to Jumièges to pray for the Duke's safety. What joy for them to know that their prayers have been granted!"

Osmond, however, could scarcely rejoice, so alarmed was he at the extreme weariness and exhaustion of his charge, who, when they brought him into the Castle hall, hardly spoke or looked, and could not eat. They carried him up to Alberic's bed, where he tossed about restlessly, too tired to sleep.

"Alas! alas!" said Osmond, "I have been too hasty. I have but saved him from the Franks to be his death by my own **imprudence**."

"Hush! Sieur de Centeville," said the Seneschal's wife, coming into the room. "To talk in that manner is the way to be his death, indeed. Leave the child to me–he is only over-weary."

Osmond was sure his Duke was among friends, and would have been glad to trust him to a woman; but Richard had but one instinct left in all his weakness and exhaustion–to cling close to Osmond, as if he felt him his only friend and protector; for he was, as yet, too much worn out to understand that he was in Normandy and safe. For two or three hours, therefore, Osmond and the Seneschal's wife watched on each side of his bed, soothing his restlessness, until at length he became quiet, and at last dropped sound asleep.

Part Three

The sun was high in the heavens when Richard awoke. He turned on his straw-filled crib, and looked up. It was not the tapestried walls of his chamber at Laon that met his opening eyes, but the rugged stone and tall loop-hole window of a turret chamber. Osmond de Centeville lay on the floor by his side, in the sound sleep of one overcome by long watching and weariness. And what more did Richard see?

It was the bright face and sparkling eyes of Alberic de Montémar, who was leaning against the foot of his bed, gazing earnestly, as he watched for his waking. There was a cry– "Alberic! Alberic!" "My Lord! my Lord!" Richard sat up and held out both arms, and Alberic flung himself into them. They hugged each other, and uttered broken exclamations and screams of joy, enough to have awakened any sleeper but one so wearied out as Osmond.

"And is it true? Oh, am I really in Normandy again?" cried Richard.

"Yes, yes!–oh, yes, my Lord! You are at Montémar. Everything here is yours. **The bar-tailed hawk** is quite well, and my mother will be here this evening; she let me ride [ahead] the instant we heard the news."

"We rode long and late, and I was very weary," said Richard, "but I don't care, now we are at home. But I can hardly believe it! Oh, Alberic, it has been very dreary!"

"See here, my Lord!" said Alberic, standing by the window. "Look here, and you will know you are at home again!"

Richard bounded to the window, and what a sight met his eyes! The Castle court was thronged with men-at-arms and horses, the morning sun sparkling on many a burnished hauberk and tall conical helmet, and above them waved many a banner and **pennon** that Richard knew full well. "There! there!" he shouted aloud with glee. "Oh, there is the horseshoe of Ferrières! And there the chequers of Warenne! Oh, and best of all, there is–there is our own red pennon of Centeville! O Alberic! Alberic! is Sir Eric here? I must go down to him!"

"Bertrand sent out notice to them all, as soon as you came, to come and guard our Castle," said Alberic, "lest the Franks should pursue you; but you are safe now–safe as Norman spears can make you–thanks be to God!"

"Yes, thanks to God!" said Richard, crossing himself and kneeling reverently for some minutes, while he repeated his Latin prayer; then, rising and looking at Alberic, he said, "I must thank Him, indeed, for he has saved Osmond and me from the cruel King and Queen, and I must try to be a less hasty and overbearing boy than I was when I went away; for I vowed that so I would be, if ever I came back. Poor Osmond, how soundly he sleeps! Come, Alberic, show me the way to Sir Eric!"

And, holding Alberic's hand, Richard left the room, and descended the stairs to the Castle hall. Many of the Norman knights and barons, in full armour, were gathered there; but Richard looked only for one. He knew Sir Eric's grizzled hair, and blue inlaid armour, though his back was towards him, and in a moment, before his entrance had been perceived, he sprang towards him, and, with outstretched arms, exclaimed: "Sir Eric–dear Sir Eric, here I am! Osmond is safe! And is Fru Astrida well?"

The old Baron turned. "My child!" he exclaimed, and clasped him in his mailed arms, while the tears flowed down his rugged cheeks. "Blessed be God that you are safe, and that my son has done his duty!"

"And is Fru Astrida well?"

"Yes, right well, since she heard of your safety. But look round, my Lord; it befits not a Duke to be clinging thus round an old man's neck. See how many of your true vassals be here, to guard you from the villain Franks."

Richard stood up, and held out his hand, bowing courteously and acknowledging the greetings of each bold baron, with a grace and readiness he certainly had not when he left Normandy. He was taller too; and though still pale, and not dressed with much care (since he had hurried on his clothes with no help but Alberic's)–though his hair was rough and disordered, and the scar of the burn had not yet faded from his cheek–yet still, with his bright blue eyes, glad face, and upright form, he was a princely, promising boy, and the Norman knights looked at him with pride and joy, more especially when, unprompted, he said: "I thank you, gallant knights, for coming to guard me. I do not fear the whole French host now I am among my own true Normans."

Sir Eric led him to the door of the hall to the top of the steps, that the men-at-arms might see him; and then such a shout rang out of "Long live Duke Richard!"– "Blessings on the little Duke!"–that it echoed and came back again from the hills around–it pealed from the old tower–it roused Osmond from his sleep–and, if anything more had been wanting to do so, it made Richard feel that he was indeed in a land where every heart glowed with loyal love for him.

Before the shout had died away, a bugle-horn was heard winding before the gate; and Sir Eric, saying, "It is the Count of Harcourt's note," sent Bertrand to open the gates in haste, while Alberic followed, as Lord of the Castle, to receive the Count.

Part Four

The old Count rode into the court, and to the foot of the steps, where he dismounted, Alberic holding his stirrup. He had not taken many steps upwards before Richard came voluntarily to meet him (which he had never done before), held out his hand, and said, "Welcome, Count Bernard, welcome. Thank you for coming to guard me. I am very glad to see you once more."

"Ah, my young Lord," said Bernard, "I am right glad to see you out of the clutches of the Franks! You know friend from foe now, methinks!"

"Yes, indeed I do, Count Bernard. I know you meant kindly by me, and that I ought to have thanked you, and not been angry, when you reproved me. Wait one moment, Sir Count; there is one thing that I promised myself to say if ever I came safe to my own dear home. Walter–Maurice–Jeannot–all you of my household, and of Sir Eric's–I know, before I went away, I was often no good Lord to you; I was passionate, and proud, and overbearing; but God has punished me for it, when I was far away among my enemies, and sick and lonely. I am very sorry for it, and I hope you will pardon me; for I will strive, and I hope God will help me, never to be proud and passionate again."

"There, Sir Eric," said Bernard, "you hear what the boy says. If he speaks it out so bold and free, without bidding, and if he holds to what he says, I doubt it not that he shall not grieve for his journey to France, and that we shall see him, in all things, such a Prince as his father of blessed memory."

"You must thank Osmond for me," said Richard, as Osmond came down, awakened at length. "It is Osmond who has helped me to bear my troubles; and as to saving me, why he flew away with me even like an old eagle with its eaglet. I say, Osmond, you must ever after this wear a pair of wings on shield and pennon, to show how well we managed our flight."

"As you will, my Lord," said Osmond, half asleep; "but 'twas a good long flight at a stretch, and I trust never to have to fly before your foes or mine again."

What a glad summer's day was that! Even the three hours spent in council did but renew the **relish** with which Richard visited Alberic's treasures, told his adventures, and showed the accomplishments he had learnt at Laon.

Part Five

The evening was more joyous still; for the Castle gates were opened, first to receive **Dame Yolande Montémar**, and not above a quarter of an hour afterwards, the drawbridge was lowered to admit the followers of Centeville; and in front of them appeared Fru Astrida's own high cap. Richard made but one bound into her arms, and was clasped to her breast; then held off at arm's-length, that she might see how much he was grown, and pity his scar; then hugged closer than ever: but, taking another look, she declared that Osmond left his hair like **King Harald Horrid-locks**; and, drawing an ivory comb from her pouch, began to pull out the thick tangles, hurting him to a degree that would once have made him rebel, but now he only fondled her the more.

As to Osmond, when he knelt before her, she blessed him, and sobbed over him, and blamed him for over-tiring her darling, all in one; and assuredly, when night closed in and Richard had, as of old, told his beads beside her knee, the happiest boy in Normandy was its little Duke.

Narration and Discussion

Is it surprising that nobody from Laon seems to have chased after Osmond and Richard? What might that mean?

Notice how Richard addresses the Norman nobles, including Count Bernard. Why do they look at him "with pride and joy?"

Creative narration: "Richard visited Alberic's treasures, told his adventures, and showed the accomplishments he had learnt at Laon." Could you act this out, or draw pictures to show the story as Richard might have told it to his friend?

For further thought: Richard is not yet completely "home," but at least he is safe in the house of his friends. What is the best thing about coming home? Can you think of any other stories you have read about people who are happy to be safely home at last? (*Heidi*, by Johanna Spyri, comes to mind, and is on the Year Two Free Reading list.)

"If they were willing to let you stay, why did you not remain where you were better off than at home?"

"Because I would a thousand times rather be with grandfather on the mountain than anywhere else in the world." (*Heidi*)

Chapter Nine: Bluetooth to the Rescue (Part 1)

Introduction

When: Some time after the previous chapter

Where: The castle of Senlis (outside of Normandy), where Richard has been sent for safety

News comes that King Louis has assembled an army and has marched into Normandy, forcing the surrender of Rouen. Ships from Denmark arrive to help the Normans, and Osmond goes to join the battle

Vocabulary

frontier: border

abode: place to live

would fain have had it supposed: wanted people to think

armourer: one who makes armour and weapons

forge: a shop where metal is worked

deemed: thought

varlet: scoundrel

I gauge my life: I am very sure

garrison: fort, castle

keel: a ship, such as **Harald Bluetooth's Long Serpent**

politic: sneaky, wily

"win my spurs": gain my knighthood

their principal resort: where they spent most of their time

People, Places, Events

King Harald: This is not King Harald from *Viking Tales* (if you recall, he was an ancestor of Richard's). This is said to be **Harald Bluetooth** or **Bluetooth**, who ruled over Denmark from 958-986 A.D. (For those who enjoy trivia, Bluetooth technology takes its name from him.) As has been stated elsewhere, historians have sometimes confused Harald with the Viking ruler **Hagrold**, who would have been more likely to have had contact with Duke Richard. However, in this story they are the same person.

Castle of Coucy: The Château de Coucy is located in Picardy, in northern France.

Senlis: the location of another castle, also in northern France (where Richard's uncle, Count Hubert, was ruler)

Reading

Part One

Montémar was too near the **frontier** to be a safe **abode** for the little Duke. His uncle, Count Hubert of Senlis, agreed with Bernard the Dane that he would be more secure beyond the limits of his own duchy, which was likely soon to be the scene of war; and, sorely against his will, he was sent in secret, under a strong escort, first to the **Castle of Coucy**, and afterwards to **Senlis**.

His consolation was, that he was not again separated from his friends: Alberic, Sir Eric, and even Fru Astrida, accompanied him, as well as his constant follower, Osmond. Indeed, the Baron would hardly bear that he should be out of his sight; and he was still so carefully watched, that it was almost like a captivity. Never, even in the summer days, was he allowed to go beyond the Castle walls; and his guardians **would fain have had it supposed** that the Castle did not contain any such guest.

Osmond did not give him so much of his company as usual, but was always at work in the **armourer's forge**–a low, vaulted chamber, opening into the Castle court. Richard and Alberic were very curious to know what he did there; but he fastened the door with an iron bar, and they were forced to content themselves with listening to the strokes of the hammer, keeping time to the voice that sang out, loud and cheerily, the song of "Sigurd's sword, and the maiden sleeping within the ring of flame." Fru Astrida said Osmond was quite right–no good weapon-smith ever toiled with open doors; and when the boys asked him questions as to his work, he only smiled, and said that they would see what it was when the call to arms should come.

They thought it near at hand, for tidings came that Louis had assembled his army, and marched into Normandy to recover the person of the young Duke, and to seize the country. No summons, however, arrived, but a message came instead, that Rouen had been surrendered into the hands of the King. Richard shed indignant tears. "My father's Castle! My own city in the hands of the foe! Bernard is a traitor then! None shall hinder me from so calling him. Why did we trust him?"

"Never fear, Lord Duke," said Osmond. "When you come to the years of Knighthood, your own sword shall right you, in spite of all the false Danes, and falser Franks, in the land."

"What! you too, son Osmond? I **deemed** you carried a cooler brain than to miscall one who was true to Rollo's race before you or yon **varlet** were born!" said [Sir Eric].

"He has yielded my dukedom! It is mis-calling to say he is aught but a traitor!" cried Richard. "Vile, treacherous, favour-seeking–"

"Peace, peace, my Lord," said [Sir Eric]. "Bernard has more in that wary head of his than your young wits, or my old ones, can unwind. What he is doing I may not guess, but **I gauge my life** his heart is right."

Part Two

Richard was silent, remembering he had been once unjust; but he grieved heartily when he thought of the French [now living] in Rollo's tower, and it was further reported that the King was about to share Normandy among his French vassals. A fresh outcry broke out in the little **garrison** of Senlis, but Sir Eric still persisted in his trust in his friend Bernard, even when he heard that Centeville [*his land*] was marked out as the prey of the [*omission*] French Count who had served for a hostage at Rouen.

"What say you now, my Lord?" said he, after a conference with a messenger at the gate. "The Black Raven has spread its wings. Fifty **keels** are in the Seine, and **Harald Bluetooth's Long Serpent** at the head of them."

"The King of Denmark! Come to my aid!"

"Aye, that he is! Come at Bernard's secret call, to right you, and put you on your father's seat. Now call honest Harcourt a traitor, because he gave not up your fair dukedom to the flame and sword!"

"No traitor to me," said Richard, pausing.

"No, verily, but what more would you say?"

"I think, when I come to my dukedom, I will not be so **politic**," said Richard. "I will be an open friend or an open foe."

"The boy grows too sharp for us," said Sir Eric, smiling, "but it was spoken like his father."

"He grows more like his blessed father each day," said Fru Astrida.

"But the Danes, father, the Danes!" said Osmond. "Blows will be passing now. I may join the host and **win my spurs**?"

"With all my heart," returned the Baron, "so my Lord here gives you leave: would that I could leave him and go with you. It would do my very spirit good but to set foot in a Northern keel once more."

"I would fain see what these men of the North are," said Osmond.

"Oh!" [said Sir Eric], "they are only Danes, not Norsemen, and there are no Vikings, such as once were when Ragnar laid waste–"

"Son, son, what talk is this for the child's ears?" broke in Fru Astrida, "are these words for a Christian Baron?"

"Your pardon, mother," said the grey warrior, in all humility, "but my blood thrills to hear of a Northern fleet at hand, and to think of Osmond drawing sword under a Sea-King."

Part Three

The next morning, Osmond's steed was led to the door, and such men-at-arms as could be spared from the garrison of Senlis were drawn up in readiness to accompany him. The boys stood on the steps, wishing they were old enough to be warriors, and wondering what had become of him, until at length the sound of an opening door startled them, and there, in the low archway of the smithy, the red furnace glowing behind him, stood Osmond, clad in bright steel, the links of his hauberk reflecting the light, and on his helmet a pair of golden wings, while the same device adorned his long pointed kite-shaped shield.

"Your wings! our wings!" cried Richard, "the bearing of Centeville!"

"May they fly after the foe, not before him," said Sir Eric. "Speed thee well, my son–let not our Danish cousins say we learn Frank graces instead of Northern blows."

With such farewells, Osmond quitted Senlis, while the two boys hastened to the battlements to watch him as long as he remained in view.

The highest tower became **their principal resort**, and their eyes were constantly on the heath where he had disappeared; but days passed, and they grew weary of the watch, and betook themselves to games in the Castle court.

Narration and Discussion

"An open friend or an open foe." Duke Richard is angry at first at the thought of Count Bernard agreeing to surrender the city of Rouen to the French. Later he understands that Bernard was setting a trap for the French, because the Danish ships were already coming down the river to fight for Normandy. While Richard is grateful for Bernard's loyalty, and hopes the battle will be a success, he doesn't think he would like to imitate his sort of cleverness. Are you like Bernard, enjoying big risky deals and maybe a bit of trickery, or more like Richard (and Duke William), preferring honesty and kindness? (There might be a need for both!)

For further thought (and this is a big one): Sir Eric admits that "my blood thrills to hear of a Northern fleet at hand," but Fru Astrida is not too impressed with that. Duke Richard made a vow to his father not to seek revenge or pay back evil for evil—but is this battle a different thing?

For further exploration: How do you think Osmond learned to make such good armour? Are you surprised that he has this hidden talent? What kinds of things do you already know how to make? Is there something that you would like to try making? How might you learn to do that?

Chapter Nine: Bluetooth to the Rescue (Part 2)

Introduction

When: Soon afterwards

Where: The castle of Senlis

Osmond returns with good news: King Louis has been taken prisoner by the Danes.

Vocabulary

warder: watchman

discomfiture: often means awkwardness or confusion, but here it means disappointment

"You will be over the battlements": You will fall over the wall

portcullis: the part of the castle gate that is raised up and down

a drooping banner [with] the golden lilies of France: Have you ever played the game called "Capture the Flag," where the goal is for one team get hold of the other team's flag? This is a real-life version: Osmond has gotten hold of the French flag, which proves that the

Normans and their Danish allies have won the battle.

I could not pledge them in a skull-goblet–set in gold though it were: I find them a little too violent for comfort

standard: a flag which was meant to stand in one place (hence its name), especially during a battle, or to mark where a king or noble was, for instance during a ceremony.

hand-and-glove: best buddies

prevail: succeed

spoils: loot, treasure

no true Norman could bear the sight of him: for various reasons, but mainly because they blamed him for the death of Duke William

hosts: armies

indifferent: not very good

People, Places, Events

Montreuil: see note in Chapter One, Part 2

Dive (pronounced "deev"): A river in western France

Reading

Part One

One day, Alberic, in the character of a Dragon, was lying on his back, panting hard so as to be supposed to cast out volumes of flame and smoke at Richard, the Knight, who with a stick for a lance, and a wooden sword, was waging fierce war; when suddenly the Dragon paused, sat up, and pointed towards the **warder** on the tower. His horn was at his lips, and in another moment, the blast rang out through the Castle.

With a loud shout, both boys rushed headlong up the turret stairs, and came to the top so breathless, that they could not even ask the warder what he saw. He pointed, and the keen-eyed Alberic exclaimed, "I see! Look, my Lord, a speck there on the heath!"

"I do not see! where, oh where?"

"He is behind the hillock now, but–oh, there again! How fast he comes!"

"It is like the flight of a bird," said Richard, "fast, fast–"

"If only it be not flight in earnest," said Alberic, a little anxiously [*omission*].

"No, young Sir," said the warder, "no fear of that. I know how men ride when they flee from the battle."

"No, indeed, there is no **discomfiture** in the pace of that steed," said Sir Eric, who had by this time joined them.

"I see him clearer! I see the horse," cried Richard, dancing with eagerness, so that Sir Eric caught hold of him, exclaiming, "**You will be over the battlements**! hold still! better hear of a battle lost than that!"

"He [has something] in his hand," said Alberic.

"A banner or pennon," said the warder; "methinks he rides like the young Baron."

"He does! My brave boy! He has done good service," exclaimed Sir Eric, as the figure became more developed. "The Danes have seen how we train our young men."

"His wings bring good tidings," said Richard. "Let me go, Sir Eric, I must tell Fru Astrida."

Part Two

The drawbridge was lowered, the **portcullis** raised, and as all the dwellers in the Castle stood gathered in the court, in rode the warrior with the winged helm, bearing in his hand **a drooping banner**; lowering it as he entered, it unfolded, and displayed, trailing on the ground at the feet of the little Duke of Normandy, **the golden lilies of France**.

A shout of amazement arose, and all gathered round him, asking hurried questions. "A great victory–the King a prisoner–**Montreuil** slain!"

Richard would not be denied holding his hand, and leading him to the hall, and there, sitting around him, they heard his tidings. His father's first question was, what he thought of their kinsmen, the Danes?

"Rude comrades, father, I must own," said Osmond, smiling, and shaking his head. "**I could not pledge them in a skull-goblet–set in gold though it were**."

"None the worse warriors," said Sir Eric. "Aye, aye, and you were dainty, and brooked not the hearty old fashion of tearing the whole sheep to pieces. You must needs cut your portion with the fine French knife at your girdle."

Osmond could not see that a man was braver for being a savage, but he held his peace; and Richard impatiently begged to hear how the battle had gone, and where it had been fought.

"On the bank of the **Dive**," said Osmond. "Ah, father, you might well call old Harcourt wary–his name might better have been Fox-heart than Bear-heart! He had sent to the Franks a message of distress, that the Danes were on him in full force, and to pray them to come to his aid."

"I trust there was no treachery. No foul dealing shall be wrought in my name," exclaimed Richard, with such dignity of tone and manner, as made all feel he was indeed their Duke, and forget his tender years.

"No, or should I tell the tale with joy like this?" said Osmond. "Bernard's view was to bring the Kings together, and let Louis see you had friends to maintain your right. He sought but to avoid bloodshed."

"And how chanced it?"

"The Danes were encamped on the Dive, and so soon as the French came in sight, Bluetooth sent a messenger to Louis, to [command] him to [go home] and leave [Normandy] to you, its lawful owner. Thereupon, Louis, hoping to win him over with wily words, invited him to hold a personal conference."

"Where were you, Osmond?"

"Where I had scarce patience to be. Bernard had gathered all of us honest Normans together, and arranged us beneath that **standard** of the King, as if to repel his Danish inroad. Oh, he was, in all seeming, **hand-and-glove** with Louis, guiding him by his counsel, and, verily, seeming his friend and best adviser! But in one thing he could not **prevail**. That ungrateful recreant, Herluin of Montreuil, came with the King, hoping, it seems, to get his share of our **spoils**; and when Bernard advised the King to send him home, since **no true Norman**

could bear the sight of him, the hot-headed Franks vowed no Norman should hinder them from bringing whom they chose. So a tent was set up by the riverside, wherein the two Kings, with Bernard, Alan of Brittany, and Count Hugh, held their meeting.

"We all stood without, and the two **hosts** began to mingle together, we Normans making acquaintance with the Danes. There was a red-haired, wild-looking fellow, who told me he had been with Anlaff in England, and spoke much of the doings of Hako in Norway; when, suddenly, he pointed to a Knight who was near [*omission*] and asked me his name. My blood boiled as I answered, for it was Montreuil himself! 'The cause of your Duke's death!' said the Dane. 'Ha, ye Normans are fallen sons of Odin, to see him yet live!'"

"You said, I trust, my son, that we follow not the laws of Odin?" said Fru Astrida.

"I had no space for a word, grandmother; the Danes took the vengeance on themselves. In one moment they rushed on Herluin with their axes, and the unhappy man was dead. All was tumult; every one struck without knowing at whom, or for what. Some shouted, '*Thor Hulfe*!' some '*Dieu aide*!' others '*Montjoie St. Denis*!' Northern blood against French, that was all our guide. I found myself at the foot of this standard, and had a hard combat for it; but I bore it away at last."

"And the Kings?"

"They hurried out of the tent, it seems, to rejoin their men. Louis mounted, but you know of old, my Lord, he is but an **indifferent** horseman, and the beast carried him into the midst of the Danes, where King Harald caught his bridle, and delivered him to four Knights to keep. Whether he dealt secretly with them, or whether they, as they declared, lost sight of him whilst plundering his tent, I cannot say; but when Harald demanded him of them, he was gone."

"Gone! is this what you call having the King prisoner?"

"You shall hear. He rode four leagues, and met [someone] whom he bribed to hide him in the Isle of Willows. However, Bernard [found him and forced him] to come out of his hiding-place, and the King is now fast guarded in Rollo's tower–[with] Danes, battle-axes on [their] shoulders, keeping guard at every turn of the stairs."

"Ha! ha!" cried Richard. "I wonder how he likes it. I wonder if he remembers holding me up to the window, and vowing that he meant me only good!"

"When you believed him, my Lord," said Osmond, slyly.

"I was a little boy then," said Richard, proudly. "Why, the very walls must remind him of his oath, and how Count Bernard said, as he dealt with me, so might Heaven deal with him."

"Remember it, my child–beware of broken vows," said Father Lucas; "but remember it not in triumph over a fallen foe. [Let everyone come] at once to the chapel, to bestow their thanksgivings where alone they are due."

Narration and Discussion

How did the calm discussions turn into a free-for-all battle (according to Osmond's story)?

A question that may come up: why was the king put into prison? The answer to that is not as simple as "he had broken the law"; he was being treated more as if he had actually been killed in the battle and lost his kingdom. (Other history sources say that he got it back some time later.)

Did the King keep the vow he made to Richard? Father Lucas (who suddenly reappears in the story) warns Richard to beware of broken vows, but also not to gloat over his "fallen foe." What does he mean?

Creative narration: You are a news reporter, and you have your choice of one person to interview: a) Osmond, b) the king, c) the red-headed Dane. Who will you choose? What might they say about the day's events?

Chapter Ten: A Norman's Courtesy (Part 1)

Introduction

When: Almost a year later

Where: The Castle of Bayeux, where Richard has returned with the de Centevilles

The two French princes arrive as hostages in Normandy. Richard tries to welcome them but cannot seem to break through their anger and fearfulness.

Vocabulary

engaged: arranged

was now allowed to ride and walk abroad freely: In Senlis, Richard had been kept almost as a prisoner, because there was so much fear for his safety.

cavalcade: procession

litter: a device used for carrying someone, like a stretcher with curtains

vouchsafing: giving

Bordeaux: a kind of wine

pasty of ortolans: bird pie

pullet: chicken

impetuous: quick to act without thinking first

maltreat: mistreat

stalwart: stubborn, strong

remonstrances: pleadings not to do something

Reading

Part One

After nearly a year's captivity, the King **engaged** to pay a ransom, and, until the terms could be arranged, his two sons were to be placed as hostages in the hands of the Normans, whilst he returned to his own domains. The Princes were to be sent to Bayeux; whither Richard had returned, under the charge of the Centevilles, and **was now allowed to ride and walk abroad freely**, provided he was accompanied by a guard.

"I shall rejoice to have Carloman, and make him happy," said Richard; "but I wish Lothaire were not coming."

"Perhaps," said good Father Lucas, "he comes that you may have a first trial in your father's last lesson, and Abbot Martin's, and return good for evil."

The Duke's cheek flushed, and he made no answer.

He and Alberic betook themselves to the watch-tower, and, by and by, saw a **cavalcade** approaching, with a curtained vehicle in the midst, slung between two horses. "That cannot be the Princes," said Alberic; "that must surely be some sick lady."

"I only hope it is not the Queen," exclaimed Richard, in dismay. "But no; Lothaire is such a coward, no doubt he was afraid to ride [*omission*]. But come down, Alberic; I will say nothing unkind of Lothaire, if I can help it."

Richard met the Princes in the court, his sunny hair uncovered, and bowing with becoming courtesy [*omission*]. With black looks, Lothaire stepped from the **litter**, took no heed of the little Duke, but, roughly calling his attendant, Charlot, to follow him, he marched into the hall, **vouchsafing** neither word nor look to any as he passed, threw himself into the highest seat, and ordered Charlot to bring him some wine.

Meanwhile, Richard, looking into the litter, saw Carloman crouching in a corner, sobbing with fright.

"Carloman!–dear Carloman!–do not cry. Come out! It is I–your own Richard! Will you not let me welcome you?" Carloman looked, caught at the outstretched hand, and clung to his neck.

"Oh, Richard, send us back! Do not let the savage Danes kill us!"

"No one will hurt you. There are no Danes here. You are my guest, my friend, my brother. Look up! here is my own Fru Astrida."

"But my mother said the Northmen would kill us for keeping you captive. She wept and raved, and the cruel men dragged us away by force. Oh, let us go back!"

"I cannot do that," said Richard; "for you are the King of Denmark's captives, not mine; but I will love you, and you shall have all that is mine, if you will only not cry, dear Carloman. Oh, Fru

Astrida, what shall I do? You comfort him–" as the poor boy clung sobbing to him.

Part Two

Fru Astrida advanced to take his hand, speaking in a soothing voice, but he shrank and started with a fresh cry of terror–her tall figure, high cap, and wrinkled face, were [frightening] to him [*omission*], and as she knew no French, he understood not her kind words. However, he let Richard lead him into the hall, where Lothaire sat moodily in the chair, with one leg tucked under him, and his finger in his mouth.

"I say, Sir Duke," said he, "is there nothing to be had in this old den of yours? Not a drop of **Bordeaux**?"

Richard tried to repress his anger at this very uncivil way of speaking, and answered, that he thought there was none, but there was plenty of Norman cider.

"As if I would taste your mean peasant drinks! I bade them bring my supper–why does it not come?"

"Because you are not master here," trembled on Richard's lips, but he forced it back, and answered that it would soon be ready, and Carloman looked imploringly at his brother, and said, "Do not make them angry, Lothaire."

"What, crying still, foolish child?" said Lothaire. "Do you not know that if they dare to cross us, my father will treat them as they deserve? Bring supper, I say, and let me have a **pasty of ortolans**."

"There are none–they are not in season," said Richard.

"Do you mean to give me nothing I like? I tell you it shall be the worse for you."

"There is a **pullet** roasting," began Richard.

"I tell you, I do not care for pullets–I will have ortolans."

"If I do not take order with that boy, my name is not Eric," muttered the Baron.

"What must he not have made our poor child suffer!" returned Fru Astrida, "but the little one moves my heart. How small and weakly he is, but it is worth anything to see our little Duke so tender to him."

"He is too brave not to be gentle," said Osmond; and, indeed, the high-spirited, **impetuous** boy was as soft and kind as a maiden, with that feeble, timid child. He coaxed him to eat, consoled him, and, instead of laughing at his fears, kept between him and the great bloodhound Hardigras, and drove it off when it came too near.

"Take that dog away," said Lothaire, imperiously. No one moved to obey him, and the dog, in seeking for scraps, again came towards him. "Take it away," he repeated, and struck it with his foot. The dog growled, and Richard started up in indignation.

"Prince Lothaire," he said, "I care not what else you do, but my dogs and my people you shall not **maltreat**."

"I tell you I am Prince! I do what I will! Ha! who laughs there?" cried the passionate boy, stamping on the floor.

"It is not so easy for French Princes to scourge free-born Normans here," said the rough voice of Walter the huntsman: "there is a reckoning for the stripe my Lord Duke bore for me."

"Hush, hush, Walter," began Richard; but Lothaire had caught up a footstool, and was aiming it at the huntsman, when his arm was caught. Osmond, who knew him well enough to be prepared for such outbreaks, held him fast by both hands, in spite of his passionate screams and struggles, which were like those of one frantic.

Sir Eric, meanwhile, thundered forth [*omission*], "I would have you to know, young Sir, Prince though you be, you are our prisoner, and shall taste of a dungeon, and bread and water, unless you behave yourself."

Either Lothaire did not hear, or did not believe, and fought more furiously in Osmond's arms, but he had little chance with the **stalwart** young warrior, and, in spite of Richard's **remonstrances**, he was carried from the hall, roaring and kicking, and locked up alone in an empty room.

"Let him alone for the present," said Sir Eric, putting the Duke aside, "when he knows his master, we shall have peace."

Narration and Discussion

Why did Louis allow his sons (both of them, in this version of the story) to be sent to Bayeux as hostages? Does that seem like a kind thing for a father to do?

Do you think Richard will be able to help Lothaire learn better behaviour?

Creative narration: What would you do if Lothaire appeared in your house, demanded fancy food, and kicked your dog? If there are enough students, they could act out either the scene from the book, or a modern-day version. A single student could also act it with an adult.

For further exploration: There have been many dinners mentioned in this book, but, aside from venison, salt beef, bread, and some possibly poisoned French food, we have heard very little about what anyone was actually eating. However, due to the popularity of both medieval festivals and castle-times school studies, there are many resources available to help you put together a medieval-style meal, or just a snack. An online article that could be useful is on a blog called "Coffee After Kids," with a post called "Family Dinner: Medieval Theme." Two foods traditionally produced and eaten in Normandy are pork and apples (including cider, as Richard mentions in this chapter).

Chapter Ten: A Norman's Courtesy (Part 2)

Introduction

When: The same night

Where: Bayeux

Richard's attempts at kindness are accepted by Carloman, but not by Lothaire.

Vocabulary

desolate: deserted, alone

crossing himself: making a gesture representing the cross of Christ; it is a blessing and sign of belief

Pater Noster: Our Father (the Lord's Prayer)

resounding: echoing

smote: struck. "His heart smote him" means he felt ashamed.

Round the fire at the lower end of the hall snored half-a-dozen men-at-arms: Castles did not typically provide bedrooms or even beds for everyone; it was common for the "lower" members of the household to find places for themselves on the floor of the great hall.

embers: small bits of glowing coal or wood in a dying fire

Reading

Part One

Here Richard had to turn, to reassure Carloman, who had taken refuge in a dark corner, and there shook like an aspen leaf, crying bitterly, and starting with fright, when Richard touched him.

"Oh, do not put me in the dungeon. I cannot bear the dark."

Richard again tried to comfort him, but he did not seem to hear or heed.

"Oh! they said you would beat and hurt us for what we did to you! but, indeed, it was not I that burnt your cheek!"

"We would not hurt you for worlds, dear Carloman; Lothaire is not in the dungeon–he is only shut up till he is good."

"It was Lothaire that did it," repeated Carloman, "and, indeed, you must not be angry with me, for my mother was so cross with me for not having stopped Osmond when I met him with the bundle of straw, that she gave me a blow, that knocked me down. And were you really there, Richard?"

Richard told his story, and was glad to find Carloman could smile at it; and then Fru Astrida advised him to take his little friend to bed. Carloman would not lie down without still holding Richard's hand, and the little Duke spared no pains to set him at rest, knowing what it was to be a **desolate** captive far from home.

"I thought you would be good to me," said Carloman. "As to Lothaire, it serves him right, that you should use him as he used you."

"Oh, no, Carloman; if I had a brother I would never speak so of him."

"But Lothaire is so unkind."

"Ah! but we must be kind to those who are unkind to us."

The child rose on his elbow, and looked into Richard's face. "No one ever told me so before."

"Oh, Carloman, not Brother Hilary?"

"I never heed Brother Hilary–he is so lengthy, and wearisome; besides, no one is ever kind to those that hate them."

"My father was," said Richard.

"And they killed him!" said Carloman.

"Yes," said Richard, **crossing himself**, "but he is gone to be in peace."

"I wonder if it is happier there, than here," said Carloman. "I am not happy. But tell me why should we be good to those that hate us?"

"Because the holy Saints were–and look at the Crucifix, Carloman. That was for them that hated Him. And, don't you know what our **Pater Noster** says?"

Poor little Carloman could only repeat the Lord's Prayer in Latin–he had not the least notion of its meaning–in which Richard had been carefully instructed by Father Lucas. He began to explain it, but before many words had passed his lips, little Carloman was asleep.

Part Two

The Duke crept softly away to beg to be allowed to go to Lothaire; he entered the room, already dark, with a pine torch in his hand, that so flickered in the wind, that he could at first see nothing, but presently beheld a dark lump on the floor.

"Prince Lothaire," he said, "here is–"

Lothaire cut him short. "Get away," he said. "If it is your turn now, it will be mine by and by. I wish my mother had kept her word, and put your eyes out."

Richard's temper did not serve for such a reply. "It is a foul shame of you to speak so, when I only came out of kindness to you–so I shall leave you here all night, and not ask Sir Eric to let you out."

And he swung back the heavy door with a **resounding** clang. But his heart **smote** him when he told his beads, and remembered what he had said to Carloman. He knew he could not sleep in his warm bed when Lothaire was in that cold gusty room. To be sure, Sir Eric said it would do him good, but Sir Eric little knew how tender the French Princes were.

So Richard crept down in the dark, slid back the bolt, and called, "Prince, Prince, I am sorry I was angry. Come out, and let us try to be friends."

"What do you mean?" said Lothaire.

"Come out of the cold and dark. Here am I. I will show you the way. Where is your hand? Oh, how cold it is. Let me lead you down to the hall fire."

Lothaire was subdued by fright, cold, and darkness, and quietly allowed Richard to lead him down. **Round the fire at the lower end of the hall snored half-a-dozen men-at-arms**; at the upper hearth there was only Hardigras, who raised his head as the boys came in. Richard's whisper and soft pat quieted him instantly, and the two little Princes sat on the hearth together, Lothaire surprised, but sullen. Richard stirred the **embers**, so as to bring out more heat, then spoke: "Prince, will you let us be friends?"

"I must, if I am in your power."

"I wish you would be my guest and comrade."

"Well, I will; I can't help it."

Richard thought his advances might have been more graciously met, and, having little encouragement to say more, took Lothaire to bed, as soon as he was warm.

Narration and Discussion

Why did Richard go out of his way to show kindness to Lothaire? Do you think the boys will begin to be friends now?

For further thought: "Why should we be good to those that hate us?" Richard tries to answer Carloman's question. If you were there with them, what would you say?

Chapter Eleven: The Passing Bell

Introduction

When: That same summer, and the autumn months

Where: Bayeux

Lothaire's attitude improves slightly, although he is still disagreeable. Carloman's delicate health worsens, and he tells Richard that he does not want to live, because the world is such a cruel place.

Warning for those who want to know these things ahead: Carloman dies at the end of this (short) chapter.

In Other News

If you are reading *Trial and Triumph*, you will be learning this week about St. Francis of Assisi, who was born about 250 years after Richard. According to *T&T*, Francis was not a "saintly-minded child" like Carloman, but spent his youth as a "fun-loving poet and singer." Perhaps that is a reminder that God can use all sorts of people!

Vocabulary

forbearance: patience

aloof: unfriendly, distant

beneficial: good

left off: stopped

sports: games

high settle: bench with a high back

draughts: drafts

Commend me to them: Send them my regards and affection

passing-bell: This is usually rung after someone dies, but here it seems to be mean that death is near.

resolution: serious decision

embalmed and lapped in lead: prepared for burial according to the customs of the time

Reading

Part One

As the Baron had said, there was more peace now that Lothaire had learnt to know that he must submit, and that no one cared for his threats of his father's or his mother's vengeance. He was very sulky and disagreeable, and severely tried Richard's **forbearance**; but there were no fresh outbursts, and, on the whole, from one week to another, there might be said to be an improvement. He could not always hold **aloof** from one so good-natured and good-humoured as the little Duke; and the fact of being kept in order could not but have some **beneficial** effect on him, after such spoiling as his had been at home.

Indeed, Osmond was once heard to say, it was a pity the boy was not to be a hostage for life; to which Sir Eric replied, "So long as we have not the training of him."

Little Carloman, meanwhile, recovered from his fears of all the inmates of the Castle excepting Hardigras, at whose approach he always shrank and trembled.

He renewed his friendship with Osmond, no longer started at the entrance of Sir Eric, laughed at Alberic's merry ways, and liked to sit on Fru Astrida's lap and hear her sing, though he understood not one word; but his especial love was still for his first friend, Duke Richard. Hand-in-hand they went about together, Richard sometimes lifting him up the steep steps, and, out of consideration for him, refraining from rough play; and Richard led him to join with him in those lessons that Father Lucas gave the children of the Castle, every Friday and Sunday evening in the Chapel. The good Priest stood on the Altar steps, with the children in a half circle round him–the son and daughter of the armourer, the huntsman's little son, the young Baron de Montémar, the Duke of Normandy, and the Prince of France, all were equal there–and together they learnt, as he explained to them the things most needful to believe; and thus Carloman **left off** wondering why Richard thought it right to be good to his enemies; and though at first he had known less than even the little leather-coated huntsman, he seemed to take the holy lessons in faster than any of them–yes, and act on them, too. His feeble health seemed to make him enter into their comfort and meaning more than even Richard; and Alberic and Father Lucas soon told Fru Astrida that [Carloman] was a saintly-minded child.

Part Two

Indeed, Carloman was more disposed to thoughtfulness, because he was incapable of joining in the **sports** of the other boys. A race round the court was beyond his strength, the fresh wind on the battlements made him shiver and cower, and loud shouting play was dreadful to him. In old times, he used to cry when Lothaire told him he must have his hair cut and be a priest; now, he only said quietly, he should like it very much, if he could be good enough.

Fru Astrida sighed and shook her head, and feared the poor child would never grow up to be anything on this earth. Great as had been the difference at first between him and Richard, it was now far greater. Richard was an unusually strong boy for ten years old, upright and broad-chested, and growing very fast; while Carloman seemed to dwindle, stooped forward from weakness, had thin pinched features, and sallow cheeks, looking like a plant kept in the dark.

The old Baron said that hardy, healthy habits would restore the puny children; and Lothaire improved in health, and therewith in temper; but his little brother had not strength enough to bear the seasoning. He pined and drooped more each day; and as the autumn came on, and the wind was chilly, he grew worse, and was scarcely ever off the lap of the kind Lady Astrida. It was not a settled sickness, but he grew weaker, and wasted away. They made up a little couch for him by the fire, with the **high settle** between it and the door, to keep off the **draughts**; and there he used patiently to lie, hour after hour, speaking feebly, or smiling and seeming pleased, when any one of those he loved approached. He liked Father Lucas to come and say prayers with him; and he never failed to have a glad look, when his dear little Duke came to talk to him, in his cheerful voice, about his rides and his hunting and hawking adventures.

Part Three

Richard's sick guest took up much of his thoughts, and he never willingly spent many hours at a distance from him, softening his step and lowering his voice, as he entered the hall, lest Carloman should be asleep.

"Richard, is it you?" said the little boy, as the young figure came round the settle in the darkening twilight.

"Yes. How do you feel now, Carloman; are you better?"

"No better, thanks, dear Richard;" and the little wasted fingers were put into his.

"Has the pain come again?"

"No; I have been lying still, musing; Richard, I shall never be better."

"Oh, do not say so! You will, indeed you will, when spring comes."

"I feel as if I should die," said the little boy; "I think I shall. But do not grieve, Richard. I do not feel much afraid. You said it was happier there than here, and I know it now."

"Where my blessed father is," said Richard, thoughtfully. "But oh, Carloman, you are so young to die!"

"I do not want to live. This is a fighting, hard world, full of cruel people; and it is peace there. You are strong and brave, and will make them better; but I am weak and fearful–I could only sigh and grieve."

"Oh, Carloman! Carloman! I cannot spare you. I love you like my own brother. You must not die–you must live to see your father and mother again!"

"**Commend me to them**," said Carloman. "I am going to my Father in heaven. I am glad I am here, Richard; I never was so happy before. I should have been afraid indeed to die, if Father Lucas had not taught me how my sins are pardoned. Now, I think the Saints and Angels are waiting for me."

He spoke feebly, and his last words faltered into sleep. He slept on; and when supper was brought, and the lamps were lighted, Fru Astrida thought the little face looked unusually pale and waxen; but he did not awake. At night, they carried him to his bed, and he was roused into a half conscious state, moaning at being disturbed. Fru Astrida would not leave him, and Father Lucas shared her watch.

Part Four

At midnight, all were wakened by the slow notes, falling one by one on the ear, of the solemn **passing-bell**, calling them to waken, that their prayers might speed a soul on its way. Richard and Lothaire were soon at the bedside. Carloman lay still asleep, his hands folded on his breast, but his breath came in long gasps. Father Lucas was praying over him, and candles were placed on each side of the bed. All was still, the boys not daring to speak or move. There came a longer breath–then they heard no more. He was, indeed, gone to a happier home–a truer royalty than ever had been his on earth.

Then the boys' grief burst out. Lothaire screamed for his mother, and sobbed out that he should die too–he must go home. Richard stood by the bed, large silent tears rolling down his cheeks, and his chest heaving with suppressed sobs.

Fru Astrida led them from the room, back to their beds. Lothaire soon cried himself to sleep. Richard lay awake, sorrowful, and in deep thought; while that scene in [the church] at Rouen returned before his eyes, and though it had passed nearly two years ago, its meaning and its teaching had sunk deep into his mind, and now stood before him more completely. "Where shall I go, when I come to die, if I have not returned good for evil?" And a **resolution** was taken in the mind of the little Duke.

Morning came, and brought back the sense that his gentle little companion was gone from him; and Richard wept again, as if he could not be consoled, as he beheld the screened couch where the patient smile would never again greet him. He now knew that he had loved Carloman all the more for his weakness and helplessness; but his grief was not like Lothaire's, for with the Prince's was still joined a selfish fear: his cry was still, that he should die too, if not set free, and violent weeping really made him heavy and ill.

The little corpse, **embalmed and lapped in lead**, was to be sent back to France, that it might rest with its forefathers in the city of Rheims; and Lothaire seemed to feel this as an additional stroke of desertion. He was almost beside himself with despair, imploring every one, in turn, to send him home, though he well knew they were unable to do so.

Narration and Discussion

If you have read the book *Understood Betsy* by Dorothy Canfield Fisher, you will remember that "Elizabeth Ann was neither very strong nor well. And as to her being happy, you can judge for yourself when you have read all this story." When she goes to live in the country, she gains strength and health, much like Lothaire in this book. Other examples of this can be found in books like *Heidi* (Free Reading in AO Year Two) and *The Secret Garden* (Year Four). Why didn't this "magic" work for Carloman?

What resolution do you think Richard has made?

Creative narration: If Richard could make a goodbye picture or card for Carloman, what might he include?

Chapter Twelve: An Oath Fulfilled (Part 1)

Introduction

When: That same autumn, shortly afterwards

Where: Falaise, "the strongest castle in Normandy"

In Other News

If you are reading Hillyer's *A Child's History of the World*, you will be reading the chapter "Bibles Made of Stone and Glass," which describes the Gothic-style churches built after Richard's time. However, Hillyer's comment that "the churches were like Bibles of stone and glass" could apply even to these earlier days. In fact, Richard's father said to him, "Bear in mind, whenever you see the Cross marked on our banner, or carved in stone on the Churches, that it speaks of forgiveness to us; but of that pardon we shall never taste if we forgive not our enemies."

If you are reading *Discovery of New Worlds* instead, you will now be up to "The Days of Chivalry."

Vocabulary

parlement: conference, meeting

you were not wont: you never used to

lamented: moaned

plover: a wading bird, but it is also seen in places like grasslands

keep: part of a castle

autumn sport: hunting

unheeding: not realizing

precipice: overhanging rock, cliff

in mortal combat: fighting to the death

People, Places, Events

Falaise Castle: also called Cliff Castle or William the Conqueror's Castle; it can still be visited.

Reading

Part One

"Sir Eric," said Richard, "you told me there was a **Parlement** to be held at **Falaise**, between Count Bernard and the King of Denmark. I mean to attend it. Will you come with me, or shall Osmond go, and you remain in charge of the Prince?"

"How now, Lord Richard, **you were not wont** to love a Parlement?"

"I have something to say," replied Richard.

The Baron made no objection, only telling his mother that the Duke was a marvellous wise child, and that he would soon be fit to take the government himself.

Lothaire **lamented** the more when he found that Richard was going away; his presence seemed to him a protection, and he fancied, now Carloman was dead, that his former injuries were about to be revenged. The Duke assured him, repeatedly, that he meant him nothing but kindness, adding, "When I return, you will see, Lothaire;" then, commending him to the care and kindness of Fru Astrida, Osmond, and Alberic, Richard set forth upon his pony, attended by Sir Eric and three men-at-arms.

Richard felt sad when he looked back at Bayeux, and thought that it no longer contained his dear little friend; but it was a fresh bright frosty morning, the fields were covered with a silvery-white coating, the flakes of hoar-frost sparkled on every bush, and the hard ground rung cheerily to the tread of the horses' feet. As the yellow sun fought his way through the grey mists that dimmed his brightness, and shone out merrily in the blue heights of the sky, Richard's spirits rose, and he laughed and shouted, as hare or rabbit rushed across the heath, or as the **plover** rose screaming above his head, flapping her broad wings across the wintry sky.

Part Two

One night they slept at a Convent, where they heard that Hugh of Paris had passed on to join the conference at Falaise. The next day they rode on, and, towards the afternoon, the Baron pointed to a sharp rocky range of hills, crowned by a tall solid tower, and told Richard, yonder was his **keep** of Falaise, the strongest Castle in Normandy.

The country was far more broken as they advanced–narrow valleys and sharp hills, each little vale full of wood, and interspersed with rocks. "A choice place for game," Sir Eric said and Richard, as he saw a herd of deer dash down a forest glade, exclaimed, "that they must come here to stay, for some **autumn sport**."

There seemed to be huntsmen abroad in the woods; for through the frosty air came the baying of dogs, the shouts and calls of men, and, now and then, the echoing, ringing notes of a bugle. Richard's eyes and cheeks glowed with excitement, and he pushed his brisk little pony on faster and faster, **unheeding** that the heavier men and horses of his suite were not keeping pace with him on the rough ground and through the tangled boughs.

Presently, a strange sound of growling and snarling was heard close at hand: his pony swerved aside, and could not be made to advance; so Richard, dismounting, dashed through some briars, and there, on an open space, beneath a **precipice** of dark ivy-covered rock, that rose like a wall, he beheld a huge grey wolf and a large dog **in mortal combat**. It was as if they had fallen or rolled down the precipice together, not heeding it in their fury. Both were bleeding, and the eyes of both glared like red fiery glass in the dark shadow of the rock. The dog lay undermost, almost overpowered, making but a feeble resistance; and the wolf would, in another moment, be at liberty to spring on the lonely child.

But not a thought of fear passed through his breast; to save the dog was Richard's only idea. In one moment he had drawn the dagger he wore at his girdle, ran to the two struggling animals, and with all his force, plunged it into the throat of the wolf, which, happily, was still held by the teeth of the hound.

Narration and Discussion

What do you think Richard might be planning to say at the conference of rulers?

Some people (like Lothaire) might think of Richard as a weakling or too "soft," with his dislike of violence. How does Richard prove here that he is not weak or cowardly?

Something to notice: At the start of the book, Richard wanted to wear a dagger, but Fru Astrida wouldn't let him. Now he is able not only to wear one, but to use it.

Creative narration: Yonge describes Richard's ride through the countryside: "It was a fresh bright frosty morning, the fields were covered with a silvery-white coating, the flakes of hoar-frost sparkled on every bush, and the hard ground rung cheerily to the tread of the horses' feet." What words here help to create a fun, happy picture for the reader? If the writer wanted to make it sound dull, sad, or frightening, how might she have changed the sentence? Here is one example:

> Overhead was a sunless sky, muffled in clouds that were heavy with snow; underfoot, a black frost; blowing over it, a wind that felt as if it would take your skin off. (C. S. Lewis, "The Hill of the Strange Trenches" in *The Silver Chair*)

Write or dictate a sentence describing something (a castle? A tree? Your breakfast?) in a joyful way, and then in a sad, annoyed, or even scary way.

Chapter Twelve: An Oath Fulfilled (Part 2)

Introduction

When: The same

Where: The same

On his way to a meeting at Falaise, Richard saves the life of a dog, and then discovers that it belongs to King Harald of Denmark.

Vocabulary

brindled: brownish, but with streaks of other colours as well

one of those Frenchified Norman gentilesse: those fancied-up Norman dudes

baldrick: belt

spent: finished, dead

I am beholden to you: I owe you something; I am grateful

tell me your boon: tell me what favour you would like

harry the fat monks of Ireland: go "a-Viking," plundering (robbing) villages etc.

recoiled: drew back

but for your clever Bonder: refers to Osmond and the way he managed to get Duke Richard away from his captors.

in transports of joy: in delight

injunction: command

People, Places, Events

Vige: the name of the dog

Jarl Richart: King Harald's way of saying "Duke Richard"

St. Clair sur Epte, which had been long in dispute: When Richard first met Alberic, he was told that Alberic's castle was in a part of Normandy that the French also claimed as their own.

Reading

Part One

The struggles relaxed, the wolf rolled heavily aside, dead; the dog lay panting and bleeding, and Richard feared he was cruelly torn. "Poor fellow! noble dog! what shall I do to help you?" and he gently smoothed the dark **brindled** head.

A voice was now heard shouting aloud, at which the dog raised and crested his head, as a figure in a hunting dress was coming down a rocky pathway, an extremely tall, well-made man, of noble features. "Ha! holla! **Vige**! Vige! How now, my brave hound?" he said in the Northern tongue, though not quite with the accent Richard was accustomed to hear. "Art hurt?"

"Much torn, I fear," Richard called out, as the faithful creature wagged his tail, and strove to rise and meet his master.

"Ha, lad! what art thou?" exclaimed the hunter, amazed at seeing the boy between the dead wolf and wounded dog. "You look like **one of those Frenchified Norman gentilesse**, with your smooth locks and gilded **baldrick**, yet your words are Norse. By the hammer of Thor! that is a dagger in the wolf's throat!"

"It is mine," said Richard. "I found your dog nearly **spent**, and I [came] to the rescue."

"You did? Well done! I would not have lost Vige for all the plunder of Italy. **I am beholden to you**, my brave young lad," said the stranger, all the time examining and caressing the hound. "What is your name? You cannot be Southern bred?"

As he spoke, more shouts came near; and the Baron de Centeville rushed through the trees holding Richard's pony by the bridle. "My Lord, my Lord!–oh, thank Heaven, I see you safe!" At the same moment a party of hunters also approached by the path, and at the head of them Bernard the Dane.

"Ha!" exclaimed he, "what do I see? My young Lord! what brought you here?" And with a hasty obeisance, Bernard took Richard's outstretched hand.

"I came hither to attend your council," replied Richard. "I have a boon to ask of the King of Denmark."

"Any boon the King of Denmark has in his power will be yours," said the dog's master, slapping his hand on the little Duke's shoulder, with a rude, hearty familiarity, that took him by surprise; and he looked up with a shade of offence, till, on a sudden flash of perception, he took off his cap, exclaiming, "**King Harald** himself! Pardon me, Sir King!"

"Pardon, **Jarl Richart**! What would you have me pardon?–your saving the life of Vige here? No French politeness for me. **Tell me your boon**, and it is yours. Shall I take you [on] a voyage, and **harry the fat monks of Ireland**?"

Richard **recoiled** a little from his new friend.

"Oh, ha! I forgot. They have made a Christian of you–more's the pity. You have the Northern spirit so strong. I had forgotten it. Come, walk by my side, and let me hear what you would ask. Holla, you Sweyn! Carry Vige up to the Castle, and look to his wounds. Now for it, young Jarl."

"My boon is, that you would set free Prince Lothaire."

"What?–the young Frank? Why, they kept you captive, burnt your face, and would have made an end of you, **but for your clever Bonder**."

"That is long past, and Lothaire is so wretched. His brother is dead, and he is sick with grief, and he says he shall die, if he does not go home."

"A good thing too for the treacherous race to die out in him! What should you care for him? he is your foe."

"I am a Christian," was Richard's answer.

"Well, I promised you whatever you might ask. All my share of his ransom, or his person, bond or free, is yours. You have only to prevail with your own Jarls and Bonders."

Richard feared this would be more difficult; but Abbot Martin came to the meeting, and took his part. Moreover, the idea of their hostage dying in their hands, so as to leave them without hold upon the King, had much weight with them; and, after long deliberation, they consented that Lothaire should be restored to his father, without ransom; but only on condition that Louis should guarantee to the Duke the peaceable possession of the country, as far as **St. Clair sur Epte, which had been long in dispute**; so that Alberic became, indisputably, a vassal of Normandy.

Part Two

Perhaps it was the happiest day in Richard's life when he rode back to Bayeux, to desire Lothaire to prepare to come with him to St. Clair, there to be given back into the hands of his father.

And then they met King Louis, grave and sorrowful for the loss of his little Carloman, and, for the time, repenting of his misdeeds towards the orphan heir of Normandy.

He pressed the Duke in his arms, and his kiss was a genuine one as he said, "Duke Richard, we have not deserved this of you. I did not treat you as you have treated my children. We will be true lord and vassal from henceforth."

Lothaire's last words were, "Farewell, Richard. If I lived with you, I might be good like you. I will never forget what you have done for me."

When Richard once more entered Rouen in state, his subjects

shouting round him **in transports of joy**, better than all his honour and glory was the being able to enter the Church of Our Lady, and kneel by his father's grave, with a clear conscience, and the sense that he had tried to keep that last **injunction**.

Narration and Discussion

What do you think of King Harald? Do you think he is serious about offering to take Richard "a-viking?"

Imagine that one of the barons says to Richard, "I see what you did there. You pretended to care about Lothaire, but really you were just trying to get rid of him." How might he respond?

How has Richard changed through the book? What were the most difficult lessons he learned?

Creative narration #1: Dramatize the scene with King Harald, or draw a picture.

Creative narration #2: What might Richard say as he kneels at his father's grave?

Conclusion

Introduction

When: Years later, when Richard is a "grey-headed man, of lofty stature and majestic bearing."

Where: The Abbey of Jumièges

Time goes by, and the author summarizes the lives of some of our characters, as far as she was able to research them.

Vocabulary

King Louis was killed by a fall from his horse: in 954 A.D. Our author has decided to give Louis no more of an ending than that; but in fact he was eventually restored to his throne, and even reconciled with Hugh the Great, before this fatal accident.

Lothaire died in early youth, and in him ended the degenerate line of Charlemagne: Actually, Lothaire (Lothair, Lothar) succeeded his father as king and reigned from 954 to 986. He was followed by his son **Louis V**, who was unfortunately known as Louis the Do-Nothing, and who died with no children of his own. So the point about Lothair being the last of the royal family is fairly accurate.

of lofty stature: tall

take sanctuary: find safety in a sacred place

one who might be my father: someone old enough to be my father

suppliant: one who requests help or mercy

wherefore art thou: why are you

own: recognize, pay homage to

Each Frenchman and each Norman vows to slay me, in revenge for your wrongs, Lord Duke: See Editor's Notes at the end of the reading

renown: fame

Where the hand of the Lord hath stricken: where God has punished

it is not for man to exact his own reckoning: it is not for man to take his own revenge

refectory: dining hall

venerable: elderly

People, Places, Events

Hugh Capet: the son of Hugh the Great, and the first king from the House of Capet (replacing the family of Louis). Also, he was Richard's brother-in-law (Richard married Hugh's sister Eumacette, also known as Emma).

Arnulf of Flanders: Count Arnulf's repentance, and Richard's forgiveness, is certainly a good ending for the story. However, he is believed to have been killed sometime later (not by Richard), in revenge for the murder of William Longsword.

Reading

Part One

Years had passed away. The oaths of Louis, and promises of Lothaire, had been broken; and Arnulf of Flanders, the murderer of Duke William, had incited them to repeated and treacherous inroads on Normandy; so that Richard's life, from fourteen to five or six-and-twenty, had been one long war in defence of his country. But [*omission*] his gallant deeds had well earned for him the title of "Richard the Fearless"–a name well deserved; for there was but one thing he feared, and that was, to do wrong.

By and by, success and peace came; and then Arnulf of Flanders, finding open force would not destroy him, three times made attempts to assassinate [Richard], like his father, by treachery. But all these had failed; and now Richard had enjoyed many years of peace and honour, whilst his enemies had vanished from his sight.

King Louis was killed by a fall from his horse; Lothaire died in early youth, and in him ended the degenerate line of Charlemagne; Hugh Capet, the son of Richard's old friend, Hugh the White, was on the throne of France, his sure ally and brother-in-law, looking to him for advice and aid in all his undertakings.

Fru Astrida and Sir Eric had long been in their quiet graves; Osmond and Alberic were among Richard's most trusty councillors and warriors. Abbot Martin, in extreme old age, still ruled the Abbey of Jumièges, where Richard, like his father, loved to visit him, hold converse with him, and refresh himself in the peaceful cloister, after the affairs of state and war.

And Richard himself was a grey-headed man, **of lofty stature** and majestic bearing. His eldest son was older than he had been himself when he became the little Duke, and he had even begun to remember his father's project, of an old age to be spent in retirement and peace.

Part Two

It was on a summer eve, that Duke Richard sat beside the white-bearded old Abbot, within the porch, looking at the sun shining with soft declining beams on the arches and columns. They spoke together of that burial at Rouen, and of the silver key; the Abbot delighting to tell, over and over again, all the good deeds and good sayings of William Longsword.

As they sat, a man, also very old and shrivelled and bent, came up to the cloister gate, with the tottering, feeble step of one pursued beyond his strength, coming to **take sanctuary**.

"What can be the crime of one so aged and feeble?" said the Duke, in surprise.

At the sight of him, a look of terror shot from the old man's eye. He clasped his hands together, and turned as if to flee; then, finding himself incapable of escape, he threw himself on the ground before him.

"Mercy, mercy! noble, most noble Duke!" was all he said.

"Rise up–kneel not to me. I cannot brook this from **one who might be my father**," said Richard, trying to raise him; but at those words the old man groaned and crouched lower still.

"Who art thou?" said the Duke. "In this holy place thou art secure, be thy deed what it may. Speak!–who art thou?"

"Dost thou not know me?" said the **suppliant**. "Promise mercy, ere thou dost hear my name."

"I have seen that face under a helmet," said the Duke. "Thou art **Arnulf of Flanders**!"

There was a deep silence.

"And **wherefore art thou** here?"

"I delayed to **own** the French King Hugh. He has taken my towns and ravaged my lands. **Each Frenchman and each Norman vows**

to slay me, in revenge for your wrongs, Lord Duke. I have been driven hither and thither, in fear of my life, till I thought of the **renown** of Duke Richard, not merely the most fearless, but the most merciful of Princes. I sought to come hither, trusting that, when the holy Father Abbot beheld my bitter repentance, he would intercede for me with you, most noble Prince, for my safety and forgiveness. Oh, gallant Duke, forgive and spare!"

Part Three

"Rise up, Arnulf," said Richard. "**Where the hand of the Lord hath stricken, it is not for man to exact his own reckoning**. My father's death has been long forgiven, and what you may have planned against myself has, by the blessing of Heaven, been brought to nought. From Normans at least you are safe; and it shall be my work to ensure your pardon from my brother the King. Come into the **refectory**: you need refreshment. The Lord Abbot makes you welcome."

Tears of gratitude and true repentance choked Arnulf's speech, and he allowed himself to be raised from the ground, and was forced to accept the support of the Duke's arm.

The **venerable** Abbot slowly rose, and held up his hand in an attitude of blessing: "The blessing of a merciful God be upon the sinner who turneth from his evil way; and ten thousand blessings of pardon and peace are already on the head of him who hath stretched out his hand to forgive and aid him who was once his most grievous foe!"

Narration and Discussion

Tell how Richard showed kindness to his worst enemy.

Yonge says that "His eldest son [Richard II, who became Duke after him, and was called "le Bon" or "The Good"] was older than he had been himself when he became the little Duke." Richard's second son, Robert, grew up to become Archbishop of Rouen. He also had other children, including a daughter, Emma, who is mentioned in Chapter 19 of *An Island Story* (read near the end of AO Year One). What things do you think Richard would teach his sons and daughters?

Editor's Note: Richard died in 996 A.D., at the age of 64. He was buried at Fécamp Abbey, which had been destroyed by Vikings, but which he had restored (as his father rebuilt Jumièges Abbey).

The Song of Finis

by Walter de la Mare

At the edge of All the Ages
  A Knight sate on his steed,
His armor red and thin with rust
  His soul from sorrow freed;
And he lifted up his visor
  From a face of skin and bone,
And his horse turned head and whinnied
  As the twain stood there alone.

No bird above that steep of time
  Sang of a livelong quest;
No wind breathed,
    Rest:
"Lone for an end!" cried Knight to steed,
  Loosed an eager rein–
Charged with his challenge into space:
  And quiet did quiet remain.

Examination Questions for *The Little Duke*, Term 2

Choose one or more of these questions to answer.

1. Tell what you know about a) Prince Lothaire, b) Prince Carloman.

2. Tell a) how Richard and Osmond escaped from Laon, or b) how Richard got to meet King Harald.

3. Tell something about Richard's life when he grew up.

End Notes

Historical Note by Charlotte Yonge

"At fourteen years of age, Richard was betrothed to Eumacette [Emma] of Paris, then but eight years old. In such esteem did Hugues la Blanc hold his son-in-law, that, on his death-bed, he committed his son Hugues Capet to his guardianship, though the Duke was then scarcely above twenty, proposing him as the model of wisdom and of chivalry.

"Richard obtained for Arnulf the restitution of Arras, and several other Flemish towns. He died eight years afterwards, in 996, leaving several children, among whom his daughter Emma is connected with English history, by her marriage, first, with Ethelred the Unready, and secondly, with Knute, the grandson of his firm friend and ally, Harald Bluetooth." [See the note about possible confusion here over names, in **Chapter Twelve**.]

"His son was Richard, called the Good; his grandson, Robert the Magnificent; his great-grandson, William the Conqueror, who brought the Norman race to England [*Our Island Story* Chapters 22-25]. Few names in history shine with so consistent a lustre as that of Richard; at first the little Duke, afterwards Richard *aux longues jambes* [of the long legs], but always Richard *sans peur* [the fearless].

"This little sketch has only brought forward the perils of his childhood, but his early manhood was likewise full of adventures, in which he always proved himself brave, honourable, pious, and forbearing. But for these our readers must search for themselves into early French history, where all they will find concerning our hero will only tend to exalt his character."

Footnotes

These are included in the original version of *The Little Duke*; but as most of them would be of little interest to students, they are omitted here.